Y0-DBK-365

Other books by Mark Kimmel

Trillion

Decimal

One

Birthing A New Civilization

Transformation

Chrysalis

ICEBREAKERS

Cosmic Paradigm

Book One

Discovering Truth

Keep up your good work
Mark

Mark Kimmel

Cosmic Paradigm

Book One

Discovering Truth

Mark Kimmel

www.cosmicparadigm.com

Paradigm Books
PO Box 538
Arroyo Grande, CA 93421
USA

88@paradigmbooks.org

To Heidi, my love, my support, my angel;
without you, this wouldn't have been possible.

CONTENTS

INTRODUCTION

I have had amazing experiences that I will now share with you. This book is about the vast Cosmic Paradigm from the vantage point of great non-physical beings. It is also about sharing what I have learned as the result of being a walk-in; receiving communications from extraterrestrials, Archangels and Ascended Masters; raising my consciousness; and experiencing the non-physical. It had to wait until I had completely set aside my prior life, as a businessman, and was fully committed to my current path as a wayshower and channel.

The Cosmic Paradigm is about non-physical beings, in collaboration with humanity, actuating the resurrection of Earth to a 12th Dimension Christed planet of Light, Love, and Unity. It is also about the massive influx of Christ Consciousness that is infusing Earth and humanity at this time. Join me, as together, we find new meaning for your life.

This book had to wait until I opened myself from my earlier life and raised my consciousness. And it had to wait until my non-physical friends assisted me to put it into words.

Many of the things I reveal in this book are very different from what is commonly known. It has taken me over twenty years to discover and then become comfortable sharing them. When you learn about them, it will open your life to new possibilities.

This book is divided into four parts: *Part I, Conventional Paradigm,* where I recount my first fifty-six years in the conventional paradigm; *Part II, Larger Picture,* where I set aside my life as a successful businessman and opened myself to a larger reality; *Part III, Communications,* where I disclose my many communications with benevolent extraterrestrials and what I learned from them; and *Part IV, Non-physical,* where I write about my interactions with great non-physical beings, how they have led me to higher consciousness, and shown me why I chose to be here, as a channel and wayshower.

I trust, by presenting things in this manner, that you will grasp the stages of my progression to higher consciousness, and see that you too can ascend to a higher energy. More importantly, I hope you will grasp the revolutionary teachings of the nonphysicals with whom I now communicate.

This book was written in cooperation with Archangel Michael, other Archangels and Ascended Masters, Adrial (a Celestial from the Andromeda Galaxy), my very special extraterrestrial friends, and great non-physical beings you will meet later. I am very grateful for the assistance of them all.

Mark Kimmel

PART I

Conventional Paradigm

Cosmic Paradigm

1

In this chapter and the next, I will show how I lived a very ordinary life for my first 56 years. I present this so that you may better understand just how radical a change I made, from my time in the conventional paradigm, to where I now am. I also present it, so you may understand just how ordinary a human I am, in many ways.

For these years, I lived as a chrysalis within a cocoon, in the conventional paradigm of the United States of America. I viewed my life, as growing up, going to college, succeeding in business, marrying, and raising a family. I took my socioeconomic environment pretty much for granted, as this was just the way things had always been, and were going to continue. In other words, I was oblivious to an alternative picture, or even the possibility thereof. I went along with the beliefs provided by my family, friends, school, religion, business associates, and the media.

During those years, my thoughts, emotions, and behavior were largely driven by anger, insecurity, judgment, feelings of less-than, and hating my body. Growing up Catholic, I had guilt about many things. Religion played an important part in forming who I was, from accepting it as a child, to rejecting it as an adult.

However, and more importantly, my life had no real meaning, no direction, other than what had been programmed into me by those embracing the values of the conventional paradigm. During most of this time I had a belief in God that was supplied by others.

There was scant consideration of a God of the larger universe, except in the fuzziest of terms.

Journey with me, now, to explore the cocoon that defined my life, from the time I was born through college. Looking back from my current perspective, I see that I neither acknowledged, nor sensed, the soul exchange I underwent when I was eleven years old. It was not for another 65 years, that I was to learn what had happened on that fateful day, January 20, 1952. So, I went about my life in the cocoon, as prescribed for a boy in the conventional paradigm. After I had grown to a young man, I suspected something had happened; I attributed it to my family, but not to me personally. None of my siblings could give me a clue about the event.

I was born at Saint Joseph's Hospital in Denver, Colorado, a little less than a year before the attack on Pearl Harbor. Needless to say, the events of the war years impacted my early years. I recall being thrown against the glove compartment of our car. My mother, Gerry Clair, had fallen asleep crossing the desert, and had driven off the highway. We were on our way, from Colorado to California, to join my father.

My father, Earl "Kim," worked in Los Angeles for TWA. He had been declared unsuitable for military service, due to his back. At TWA, he worked at prioritizing seats on flights, between military and commercial flyers.

At our home in Los Angeles, I recall watching the water in the toilet bowl sloshing around, as my Mother and I endured an earthquake. I also remember the blackout shades, that covered each window to thwart a bombing by the Japanese. I walked on the sand at Long Beach with my Grandma Bee, and put my foot in the water of the ocean. Mother hated Los Angeles, particularly the earthquakes, so as soon as my father found a job in Denver, we moved back there.

Looking back at that time, I have no recollections of being hugged or kissed during my early years. I have seen an old movie, where I was paraded in new clothes and rode a tricycle. I have the distinct impression that my parents did not express love. I see myself in those early years as very shy.

I vaguely remember the first house in which we lived, on Quitman Street in Denver, Colorado. I remember the sandbox in the back yard. My Grandma Bee lived less than a block away from us. Gramps owned a Skelly service station across the street from it.

I recall watching Grandma Bee chop off the head of a chicken, and letting it run around the yard headless. Next, she plunged the chicken into a pot of boiling water, then plucked out all its feathers. During the war years, many people had victory gardens and raised chickens in their backyards.

I recall happy times with Grandma Bee playing games, riding the streetcar to downtown Denver, dining on chicken-a-la-king at the restaurant on the top floor of the Denver Dry Goods building, and watching Ester Williams movies. She told everyone that I was her "prince charming."

I was on a street in downtown Denver when tickertape filled the sky. I asked my father what was going on. "It's the end of the war," he replied. I failed to see its significance, although it was explained to me. By that time Dad was working at Western Airlines, with an office in the Brown Palace Hotel in downtown Denver.

As a young child, I learned that Grandma Bee had a stint on the Pawnee Reservation in Kansas because her parents had died in an accident. Despite her blonde hair, she had sufficient Indian blood to be sent there. Her grandparents eventually found her, and brought her to Denver. My father's biological father abandoned the two of them, in Colorado Springs, shortly after my dad was born. Grandma Bee's sister, May, was married to Millard Drake, who hooked Bee up with his brother, Elmer Drake, Gramps. Except for Grandma Bee, no one talked about having Indian blood; my father was very intent on blending in with the majority white society.

May and Millard came to Sunday dinner at Grandma Bee's house quite often. It was usually chicken and dumplings, a big favorite of mine. The group played games often at Grandma Bee's: Pick up Sticks. Thimble, Thimble, Who's Got the Thimble? Grandma Bee had an old treadle sewing machine where she made clothes for us.

Gramps was a big help, as he knew a lot about a lot of things. He had homesteaded in New Mexico at age sixteen, raising broom straw on his one hundred twenty acres. He had been a prize fighter, before they introduced boxing gloves, had hauled coal from the mines north of Denver, and had been a sheet metal worker. He was an activist in the union. Gramps was the one who taught me to paint around windows, so carefully that not a speck of paint was out of place.

When my brother Neil was born, we moved to a larger house on Perry Street. It was a small two bedroom with one bathroom and a glassed-in porch on the rear. The house was set above a short grassed bank, back from a wide sidewalk in front. The front porch was only a bit wider than the doorway, but enough for a chair or two. Neil and I shared the second bedroom. A single car garage sat to one side of the small back yard. I remember coal being delivered to the side of the house, and my father getting up each morning, to stoke the furnace in the dark basement.

When my brother Brian was born, I was given my own room, on the back porch. This room was okay in the summer, but in the winter ice formed on the single-pane windows. I would put my foot out over the lone furnace register to get hot air up under my covers. By that time, we had switched the heating of the house to natural gas.

A long closet connected to my brothers' room. I enjoyed sneaking through it to scare them. I have few other memories of interacting with my brothers, probably because those memories belonged to the prior occupant of my physical body.

I remember going to kindergarten at Edison Grade School

and how I cried at being left alone. Later I walked to the school, about five blocks away, for six grades. I passed by Grandma Bee and Gramps' house along the way plus a candy store on the corner across from the school.

We played marbles in the playground at school, and on the carpet at home. I had my favorite agate and a bag of marbles. I had several yoyos, one with jewels on the side. There was a man who hung out around the candy store, showing us how to do tricks with our yoyos, and, of course, selling them to anyone interested.

In sixth grade, I had a crush on Margret. We played Spin the Milk Bottle at her birthday party. I was disappointed when she went away to a different junior high school. I had a number of friends, but none close. Ours was not the house where everyone congregated, so I was always visiting somewhere else.

When they served stuffed peppers at school, I was allowed to buy lunch that day; otherwise, it was bologna and white bread. Sometimes I got chopped olives and mayonnaise sandwiches. The school furnished milk with lunch.

As a child, I had lots of sinus problems, probably due to the very dry air in buildings during the winter. I spent many days at Edison with a runny nose and clogged ears. My handkerchief was dripping wet by the end of the school day. Mother was quite insistent on giving me nose drops each night. I am quite sure this was the beginning of my hearing problems.

Another time, I lay on the bed in my room as my mother placed hot compresses on my abdomen to rid me of the hernia that had been diagnosed by a doctor. These illnesses served to reinforce my low self-concept, as my mother regarded me as a sickly child.

I took piano lessons from a woman who lived a block away, and later from my aunt, who lived on the other side of Denver. I resented practicing, because I could not stand to do anything repetitiously, a trait I retain to this day. Needless to say, I never graduated beyond rudimentary playing. Many, many years later, my aunt confessed to me that I really never had the talent to be a pianist. Her son, Barry, turned out to be a very accomplished concert pianist.

Under the influence of the cold war, I spent many hours constructing model airplanes and drawing defense emplacements. I had my sight set on being an architect or designer.

Gramps had used sheet metal strips around his strawberries. I fell on one of them, gouging my leg, just below the kneecap. I recall, quite vividly, spurting blood clear across the porch of Grandma Bee's house. They rushed me to a doctor, a few blocks away. Fortunately, he was former military and knew how to treat a wound. After pouring a lot of alcohol into the wound, he stitched me up saying, "You're damn lucky. Another half inch and you would've been crippled." I still bear the scar of that incident.

My family was very Catholic and conservative. As a small tyke, I struggled to be quiet during mass, and to behave when my parents went to the front of the church. Later I was to learn that they were going to communion, to eat the body of Jesus. Later again, I made my first communion without really understanding what it was all about, despite the hours of memorizing the catechism. I did my first confession, and the bishop anointed me in the sacrament of confirmation, at Saint Dominic's Catholic Church, without really understanding the significance of it all. I recall walking, well over a mile, to attend summer catechism classes, and attending mass each Sunday and Holyday.

I memorized the Catholic Catechism, with all of its precise dogma and restrictions. It talked about the Trinity with God the Father, God the Son, and the Holy Ghost. God the Father was loving, but also very demanding and judgmental. There was heaven and hell. Jesus was God the Son. He walked the Earth to show us love and a better way to live. He was crucified to atone for our sins. It was assumed that Earth was the only inhabited planet in the universe.

My father was totally fascinated with airplanes and flying. We traveled to Tulsa, Oklahoma. Western Airlines wanted him to transfer there, to manage their operations.

From his job with Western Airlines, he took a job with a start-up, Monarch Airlines. Monarch was headquartered in Denver and flew to nearby towns. It was later merged with another small airline to form Frontier Airlines. My father was sales manager for Monarch. He originated the idea of reserved seating; it later spread to all airlines.

Dad took flying lessons, and found time to fly a small plane. He delighted in taking me, and my brothers, to watch the planes take off at Stapleton Airfield. I found airplanes of less interest than watching trains, so the family would go to the railroad yards, so I could watch the locomotives.

I saw TV for the first time in 1953 when we went to Albuquerque to visit friends of my father. We did not have television in our home until I was sixteen.

From the airlines, Dad went to work for General Tire, then had his own used car business at Colfax and Spear, in downtown Denver. He eventually wound up at Rickenbaugh Cadillac, where he was sales manager. He remained in that position all the way through my college years.

I look back at my years at Edison and see a fairly normal, if fragmented, life of a young boy. I recall it as being pretty much the same as everyone else around me. I accepted anger, drama, anxiety, and judgment as the norm. I did not see anger expressed in my family, and recall little of it in others. I recall other kids beating up on me, but only one time. Grandma Bee came to my rescue, as the altercation was on her property.

During this time, a couple of events do stand out for me: There were a number of climbing ropes in the gym at Edison. As a sixth grader I was expected to climb to the top. Despite encouragement by the teachers, I never accomplished this. My mother enrolled me in classes at the local YMCA. I was to learn to swim across the pool. I never managed to do this. My mother argued with the instructor about his failure to see my accomplishment, saying she was sure I had done it. Both of these contributed to my feelings of less than and unworthiness. To this day, I am cautious around deep water and heights, although I do enjoy body surfing.

Out of used lumber, I built a hideout in a corner of our garage, above where tools were stored. It was where I could be alone. I would climb up into it and lock the door against my little brothers.

Goody lived next door. He was a retired railroad engineer. A kindly man who flexed his large right hand, the "iron claw," when he wanted to tease us.

I recall my father throwing the ball to me in our backyard. He was very patient, as I developed little or no skill at throwing or catching a ball. Later, when my folks offered to get me into Little League baseball, I refused to participate. I had no interest in organized sports, and subsequently participated in very few.

I did enjoy reading, especially Zane Grey and other western novels. This was my pastime, when I contracted some sort of a foot disease, that the doctors said came from the jungles of Southeast Asia. I had to sit for hours, on the front porch of our house on Perry Street, my feet in a bucket of purple liquid.

I was analyzed by a school counselor at Edison; he was worried about my depression, and lack of interactions with others. He recommended that I start following sports, so I would have something to talk about. I said I had no interest in them. He also told me I had flat feet, which I have subsequently determined that I do not have. Growing up during that time, I fortunately escaped the drugs that are administered today to kids who are judged to be depressed.

I have good memories of going to a number of Denver Bears baseball games with Grandma Bee and Gramps. Currently, I enjoy following the USC and Colorado football teams and Colorado Rockies baseball. In years past, I was an accomplished skier, and a ski instructor; today I play pickleball several times a week. These accomplishments at sports have served to buoy my self-confidence, compared to where I was as a child.

In many ways my father was very good to me, in that we did a lot of things together. I recall flying kites at Sloan's Lake Park, a few blocks away, and ice skating on that lake during the coldest months. My father loved fly fishing more than almost anything; so I learned to fish from an early age.

I remember going fishing with dad, Gramps, Neil and Brian along the South Platte River. Gramps had made cots from iron pipes and canvas. We had an Army surplus tent and sleeping bags. Cooking over an open fire was great, particularly the marshmallows. I recall catching a number of sucker fish because my bait was dragging along the bottom of the river. We threw the suckers onto the river bank, and took a number of trout home.

Another time, we all went to Woods Lake, a resort high in the mountains south of Eagle, Colorado. This was a very special place, with streams and lakes loaded with trout. We slept in cabins. By that time, I was adept enough with fly fishing to catch my limit, as did everyone else. A few years later, my family, along with other relatives, considered buying the resort, but could not afford the price. Eventually, it was sold to a group of wealthy people from Aspen.

Another time I recall fishing with my two brothers and dad at Gross Reservoir, in the mountains west of Boulder. We did not have much luck that day. However, on the drive home we all got to laughing, at something so hard that we had to stop the car. This stands out for me as a very rare emotional expression for my family.

My dad and I played chess frequently, as we listened to music from his new Grundig radio and record player. We played poker at every family gathering, as soon as the dishes were cleared. My dad worked very hard at supporting his family; Mom was a stay at home mother, with eventually five children.

One incident stands out for me. Friends of our family lived a block away. One day, without prior notice or training, I was told to put on boxing gloves. Jan, a year older and later to become a top policeman in Denver, and I squared off. Everyone thought it was great fun to watch me trying to escape his punches. They even took a movie of it.

I do not recall any encouraging words from either parent, when I brought home report cards. I was never good enough in their eyes. As the oldest, they expected much of me. My father believed his role was to challenge me. I do not recall him ever saying that he loved me.

My mother was young when she gave birth to me. I have been told that there was a prior birth, a brother, who did not survive. This made my folks doubly cautious and tentative with me. I have been told that my mother followed Dr. Spock to the letter. I was not nursed, rather I was fed with a bottle, and only at specified times, regardless of my crying. I had colic for my first year.

Years later, during one of my many psychotherapy sessions, I was asked to draw a picture of my mother and myself. I drew a picture of her changing my diaper, as she stood arm's length away, holding her nose. I do not recall her holding me, or saying that she loved me. I am quite sure this imprinted my psyche with an impression of what a mother was like.

I have had a hard time forgiving my mother, for how she distanced herself. Yes, I know that was part of the behavior of that generation, but it has not made it any easier for me. As I type these words, I am forgiving her for all that I may have projected on her. I know that she did the very best with what she had to give. Thank you, Mom, for everything.

On January 20, 1952, I underwent a soul exchange. By prior arrangement, the soul that had come into my physical body at birth agreed to leave my body. I, the new soul, "walked-in" to the physical body of an eleven-year-old boy, soon to turn twelve.

My mother undoubtedly noticed a change in me, but had no

point of reference. She and I never spoke of it. For my part, I withdrew and became even more shy, as I sought to fit into my new physical form. I now know that I had come from the Andromeda Galaxy, a 15th Dimension galaxy. There I had been used to a semi-physical form, and functioning at a much higher level of consciousness. So, I did whatever was asked of me, as I sought to fit into my new family, my environment, and the belief system around me.

My memories of the years before my walk-in are less complete than my memories subsequent to that event. The details of those earlier memories belong to the prior soul, who walked-out of my physical body.

Other walk-ins have taken place concurrent with a traumatic physical event, such as an accident. Other walk-ins recount all the memories they have of their prior life, before entering the new physical body. Other walk-ins talk about the emotional turmoil that accompanied adjusting to a new body. I recall nothing like this. I stuffed my emotional reactions, and became quite depressed, as a way to cope with living in a totally new environment, with a new family, and in a new physical body. This is the way in which the former occupant of my body, and his family, traditionally dealt with everything. It is only now, as I write these words, that I am able to get in touch with some of the trauma of the early years of this experience.

From my current vantage point, I can see that I choose this particular body and family, so that the higher consciousness imprint I was carrying could be firmly seated in the conventional paradigm. This to give me an empathy with what life is like for Earth humans.

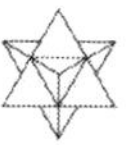

I attended Lake Junior High for one semester after graduating from 6th grade at Edison in January. I walked a little over a mile from our home on Perry Street each day, usually with a friend, Hal. I recall only one teacher during that time, a small man who wore a bow tie and taught math. He was really tough. I learned a lot.

One day we were lined up for some event and there were some Mexican kids just in back of me. They started to tease me. I turned around, and planted a punch on the jaw of the leader. He collapsed on the floor. That immediately started the other Mexican kids insisting that I show up after school to engage them. I was totally surprised at my action, and I was very afraid of what was going to happen when I showed up.

I did show up, with a friend, at the appointed time and place. No one was there. On the way home, this same guy wanted to get into a fight with me, so I could prove how tough I was. I declined. This is the only instance in which I have ever physically assaulted another person.

As a teenage boy, I had lots of sexual fantasies, and managed to smuggle a *Playboy* magazine into my room. My mother found it. She promised not to say anything to Dad, if I would throw it away immediately. This did not stop my habit of arousing myself. I felt guilty about it, and confessed it to a priest regularly. Monsignor Flannigan explained, to a group of us eighth grade boys, that our genitals were just a bunch of nerves and muscles, and not to let them distract us from being good Catholic boys. From the moment of my first ejaculation, I knew that I was doing something wrong, that it was a sin. I dutifully confessed each week, but my sexual energy was such that I did not stop. As a good Catholic boy, this fed my guilt and contributed to my low self-esteem. I remember walking the stations of the cross, and saying my rosary, as penance.

I was not at all attracted to the girls in my class at St. Mary Magdalene School, where I spent seventh and eighth grades under the dominations of the nuns. They always paired me with Jane, because we were the tallest in the class. I did have a few neighborhood friends who were not Catholic; it was from them that I learned about sex. One of them had a girlfriend, with whom he engaged in heavy petting. I listened as another friend talked dirty to a girl on the phone.

As I have grown up, sex remains an element in my life. I have been with a number of women, always with love for them and appreciation. As I observe other men in this culture, many use sex as a means of domination over women. I am sensitive to domination, verbal or physical. This is probably due to the imprinting of my soul, from my many years in the energy of Andromeda.

When my sister Kay was on the horizon, my folks bought a house on West 32nd Avenue, a walk-out ranch near the highest point in Denver, and not far from Elitch Gardens, an amusement park with its roller coaster and other rides. From the front, the house appears to be a modest single story yellow brick with a red shingle roof. From the window in the living room, I could look south seventy miles to Pike's Peak in Colorado Springs. When my window was open during the summer months, I would go to sleep to the noise of Elitch's roller coaster.

I helped my dad refinish the lower level to make bedrooms for us three boys. We tore down and rebuilt walls, laid linoleum on the floors, painted, and finished it off, including new electrical and furnace ducts. I wound up with a bedroom of my own, in a corner of the downstairs, overlooking the back yard. I turned down new bedroom furniture for that room, telling my folks they could not afford it.

I had a fascination with chemicals, and made a cabinet in the garage, so I could experiment. I discovered that I could make my own firecrackers, out of a combination of magnesium and other incendiary items. By enclosing them in a container, like a pipe, I could create quite an explosion. One day I went a little too far and created a bigger bang. When my dad got home, I got spanked.

Saint Mary Magdalene School was nine blocks away from our home, so I walked on both nice days and through heavy snow. The school was new, so we were its first seventh grade class. As I recall, there were about twenty of us in the classroom.

It was there I encountered a Catholic nun, whose name I had difficulty pronouncing, and do not know how to spell. I found school very boring, especially rote memorizing. So, I took to exchanging notes with other students. This eventually led to banishment to the hall, as well as a slap or two across the knuckles with a ruler.

My acne started at about that time. The initial treatment was low-level radiation, of the type used for x-rays. I recall the smell of the x-ray machine, as it treated my skin ailment. The x-ray technician stood behind a lead shield. Then the dermatologist tried freezing my acne eruptions. The latter produced large ugly welts over my face and back. The x-ray treatments produced a long-term reaction in my body; basal cell carcinomas appear on my face, every few months.

I think my acne had to do with Saint Mary Magdalene School and my Catholic religion, which at an unconscious level I, my soul with a 15th Dimension imprint, knew was not right. My parents were good Catholics, so there were no alternatives to this school where religion was a primary subject. I do not remember much about the other subjects I was taught, but I do remember that staying with the same teacher all day was not inspiring. It was quite a transition from the public schools, where I had gone since kindergarten.

I learned to walk the Stations of the Cross, around the perimeter of the church, to relive the last minutes of the life of Jesus, and to ponder how I had sinned. There were both venial sins and mortal sins. Mortal sins, unless they were confessed and forgiven by the priest, would send you directly to hell after you died. Venial sins would direct your soul to Purgatory, where you waited until the sins had been burned away, and you were fit to go to heaven.

In the eighth grade we took an I.Q. test. When the results of the test were announced, Mike got the top score (he was headed for the priesthood). I came in second. The nun's comment in front of the class was, "You cheated. I know you did. You're not that smart."

I attended Regis High School, a Jesuit boys school about a mile away in North Denver. Until I had a car of my own, I received a ride in the morning with Mario, who lived next door. After school, I walked home, sometimes stopping off at my uncle Tom's house, where he tried to interest me in lifting weights. He had just gotten out of the Navy, and was in great physical shape. I tried it a few times, then I did not stop by any more.

At Regis, I learned Latin, in addition to all the more familiar subjects. Religion class was a daily event. Mass was at least once a week. I recall the Jesuit priests and scholastics, who taught us, as very intelligent and highly motivated. All were strict disciplinarians.

There were no physical education classes, so unless you were a member of the football or basketball team, you went without. I was on the chess team and the bowling team. It was not until I had my first automobile that I enjoyed going to football and basketball games, and cheering for the home team. Regis always had very good teams in each sport.

It was during this time that I became even more depressed. My acne became worse. I did not fit with most of the other kids, many of whom came from a wealthier section of Denver and knew each other from grade school. I only knew what girls were through stories and pictures. I barely fitted in and was very lonely. From my current perspective, I believe that my imprinting, from many years in Andromeda as a female, had a lot to do with my difficulties as a teen. I do not regret this experience, for I can now relate to people who are feeling depressed, for one reason or another.

I was sixteen years older than my younger sister, Gail. She was born while I was at Regis High School. Because of my preoccupation with school and my depression, I did not really connect with her until many years later, when we were both adults and she was living in Oakland, California.

When I asked my father why he never encouraged me, he said it was his job to challenge me to make me strong. I later learned that this verbal abuse was one of the causes of my low self-concept.

At age fourteen, I found a job at Furr Foods, to which I rode my bicycle. I started out as a bag boy, then a stock boy, and then a cashier. I worked at Furr Foods until I graduated from the University of Colorado, eventually becoming an assistant manager. People commented on my nice smile, even though acne raged across my face. My memory of my acne, during these years, was that it was the worst I had ever seen on anyone. My first car was a "robin's egg blue" 1954 Chevrolet convertible. I bought it with money I had earned at Furr's.

It was not until my senior year of high school that I had my first date. Bobett lived in a fashionable area of East Denver and attended Saint Mary's Academy, an all-girls school on the south end of Denver. I recall hours of necking, but no petting, or sexual adventures with such a good Catholic girl. Beth came along next. She was part of the east Denver crowd that attended Regis and Saint Mary's. Through friendship with her, I became one of the group who dated, drank beer, and hung out together.

My principal gains from Regis High School were the discipline of the Jesuit education and the grounding in the basics. My greatest disadvantages were the lack of physical education, and the fact that it was a boys' school. I left Regis with a low self-confidence, but a scholarship to Regis College. I turned down an arrangement whereby I could attend Dartmouth, with a loan from my dad's boss. My father was heartbroken at my decision, but I was not ready to venture into such a foreign environment, so far from home.

My high school graduation present was a trip to the West Coast with my grandparents, including stops in Las Vegas, Los Angeles, and San Francisco. There I saw a larger world than Denver. It eventually inspired me to take my first job in California, after graduating from CU Boulder.

At that time, Regis College was an all-men's school. In order to help my folks financially, I attended it for two years. There I studied physics, chemistry, English, and philosophy. Religion was, of course, mandatory. My English teacher singled out one of my compositions, to enter into a national competition.

By the time I attended Regis College, my acne was to a point that I was comfortable associating with both men and women. I dated several women from Loretto Heights College, a Catholic woman's college on the south side of Denver. Regis was a small college and it did not take long for me to feel like I knew almost everyone by name. I was friendly with the Dean of Students with whom I maintained contact for many years after leaving Regis.

The final semester of my second year at Regis College, I boarded in Carrol Hall. For me it was a welcome release from the strict life at home. My dorm room was private with a wash basin. Lavatories and showers were down the hall. It was during this time that I learned to consume large quantities of alcohol. My group stopped at Ernie's, a bar near Regis, for martinis, after our dates at Loretta Heights. Everyone had a fake I.D.

My father insisted that I study engineering because of Sputnik, even though I wanted to be an architect. "I know too many of them that are starving to death," was his comment. The same was true when I wanted to study law, rather than continue with my engineering degree. Since I was not financially independent, I followed his demands.

After two years at Regis College, where I obtained a minor in philosophy, along with my studies in physics, chemistry, religion, and English, I transferred to the University of Colorado at Boulder. There I entered into the remainder of a five-year program. I carried about twenty hours each semester, a mixture of engineering and business courses. I particularly liked marketing and small business. By the time I graduated, I had accumulated well over two hundred semester hours.

I enjoyed my business courses, and received good grades in these. I did not enjoy my engineering courses, primarily because Regis College had not prepared me for the mathematics required for them. I did receive a good foundation that in later years helped me to avoid getting "snowed" by engineers looking for venture capital financing. I recall creating a sensation one day, as I incorrectly connected a large generator producing 100 amps and melted the metal probe.

During my years at CU, I lived off-campus in three different apartments with three different roommates, all of whom I had known from my days at Regis High. One apartment was long with thin mattresses over plywood in separate tiny rooms. My final apartment, in a two-story building across from the Harvest House Hotel, is still in operation. It was filled with students in their final year. My apartment mates were Jerry and Larry, both engineering students. Two close friends, Charlie and Tom, lived a block away. We brewed beer in our storage space—not too bad and a real novelty.

Boulder was a wonderful experience, filled with football, beer and women. I soon put aside the strict teachings of my Catholic upbringing and joined in, but I never lost my connection to God. My interactions with young women were still guarded. It was not until my senior year that I had intercourse.

My second year at CU, I totaled my Chevy on the Denver-Boulder Turnpike. I was headed back to CU to take in a football game. I recall thinking, not too long before the accident happened, that I should not be happy, because whenever that happens, something bad would follow.

Distracted by two girls riding horses alongside the road, I did not stop in time to avoid a rear end collision. Fortunately, the car ahead of me had also stopped suddenly, and my front fender went under their rear fender. My skis, that had rested across the seat, went through the front window. My body busted the steering wheel. My chin got a severe gash.

Unable to find a doctor at student health services, I went to the football game with my bloody chin. Later, I got three stitches.

My next car was a dark green 1948 Pontiac coupe. I had it until my final year, when I acquired a brand new 1963 bronze Chevy Camaro. It had a rear engine with a super charger, and was deceptively quick on acceleration.

For spending money, I worked as the Business Manager of the *Colorado Daily*, the student newspaper. The pay was good enough to allow me a lifestyle of beer, girls, and an occasional fine restaurant. At the *Daily*, I supervised a paid staff of sales people, accountants, and proof readers. The editorial side of the *Daily* was involved with Students for a Democratic Society, whose demonstrations forced early retirement on the University's president. I was not particularly aware politically, but recall Bobby Kennedy and Eleanor Roosevelt coming to CU.

My final year, I wrote a weekly column for the paper under the name of Reggie Van Pen. I was invited to fraternity and sorority parties, to chronicle their good times. I also ate at local restaurants, to promote their menus. I dated a number of women during my years at CU. The only one who stands out is Victoria, a cute blonde from New York, whom I met skiing in Aspen.

Because of my heavy course load and my work at the *Colorado Daily,* I did not participate in any sports, other than skiing. On three separate occasions I rented a house in Aspen, Colorado, and had a large group of CU students camp out there. It paid for my trip and I had a grand time.

Football games were a big event at CU, on Saturdays in the fall. In those days, CU had a good team and ranked high within the league. I attended each home game and traveled to Kansas by train for one. I have maintained my interest in college football to this day, despite the obvious energy of domination that is key to this sport. Now, as long as I can visualize the players, as kids having a good time, I am not thrown back into lower level 4th Dimension.

It was during my last semester at CU that I finally found a girl who would have sex with me. It was a wonderful experience, even though it was purely physical, rather than out of love.

My last semester, a 10-week summer semester to get my final credits, I took German and small business. The small business teacher told me I would never be a success in small business, but he still gave me an "A". I dated the daughter of the German teacher, and squeaked by with a "C". I had a different date almost every night, visited Tulagi, a local night club, several times a week, and drank a pitcher of beer at the Sink on the off-nights. I graduated with two B.S. degrees: Electrical Engineering and Business, over two hundred semester hours of credits, and a very respectable grade point.

As a reward, I drove to New Jersey to meet up with Jim, a friend from CU, and spend a few days on the Jersey shore. There it was cherrystone clams on the half-shell for breakfast, along with a glass or two of beer, and nightlife until late. I drove back to Chicago for my first days at work at a convention where 3M was exhibiting.

In Summary:

I have happy, if fragmented, memories of my early childhood (the prior occupant of my body retained most of them). Both Grandma Bee and Gramps were significant factors because my mother had two other boys to occupy her and my father, who worked long hours. My father was closely connected to his mother, Grandma Bee, somewhat to the exclusion of my mother. As a result, I do not have memories of a close connection to my mother. I do not know if she sensed the changes that occurred when I walked into the physical body of her child. Dad provided me with experiences and his discipline developed skills that have served me well.

My teen years were a time of turmoil. Seen from my current perspective, as a walk-in from a prior very high consciousness in a female body, I can see why I struggled so during my teenage years and was withdrawn and shy. I can also understand my fascination with my male physical body. I have since released much of the guilt acquired from my Catholic upbringing. Another trait, that I carried from my prior life in Andromeda, was that I never felt the need to dominate others, either in personal relationships, or in sports.

By the end of college, I had come a long way from the shy, depressed child of my early years. My college years opened me to a different reality, but still within the conventional paradigm. I thoroughly enjoyed both drinking with the boys and dating women. I acquired a measure of self-confidence and a pedigree, that started me on the next chapter of my journey. This was a high water mark, that I would not see again for many years.

Whatever I had achieved thus far was within the cocoon of the conventional paradigm. Despite the good times, and my achievements, I was never far away from feelings of separation, judgment, anxiety, drama, and guilt. I had learned to cope with them, but they were buried and influencing my beliefs, emotions, thoughts, words, and actions. I saw the same in others, despite their best efforts to hide their underlying psychological and energetic foundations.

Unlike others who may have been aware of their higher selves, or had parents who encouraged alternative ways of thinking and doing, I knew very little of life beyond the conventional. As a child, I was never encouraged to explore beyond the cocoon prescribed by my parents and the Catholic church. I now believe that my soul selected this family of origin, and this path in the conventional paradigm, to create a platform from which I could show others how to move away from these traditional ways.

Looking back at this period of my life, from my current perspective of higher consciousness plus knowing that I am a walk-in, I see that these years were necessary to help me integrate into my physical body, after I had lived in the rarified higher density of Andromeda. My life in a conservative Catholic family provided stability. My father's tough stance with me served to harden me for the life ahead; while unpleasant at the time, it served to toughen a shy boy for the road ahead. Breaking away from the cocoon, in which I had grown up, was the first step towards evolving to where I now am.

2

From 1963 to 1996, I lived at the forefront of technology. First at 3M Company, then AC&C, then Motorola, and finally as a venture capitalist with my own series of venture funds. It was exciting to help men and women with new ideas and technologies bring them to fruition. I directly participated in two significant new developments of which I am proud. Nonetheless, it all took place within the conventional paradigm, where there are no fundamental changes for humanity, albeit everyone has lived more comfortably because of new technologies, and some have prospered mightily.

While I worked in the exciting climate of entrepreneurship for most of my business life, I occasionally reached outside my cocoon to involve myself in unconventional activities and events. But the cocoon enveloped me, dragging me back into insecurity, anger, judgment, and drama.

All in all, I led a very rich life, in terms of conventional experiences within the 3rd Dimension. I regret none of my experiences, even those that were painful, some the result of my bad judgment. I apologize for any hurt that I may have inflicted on others in pursuit of what I believed was best for me. I have learned as much from my failures, as from my joys and accomplishments. Though I had no inkling that I had walked-into this physical body, I now see that I was a soul learning to function in a dense physical body, enjoying every moment of the experience.

My combination of engineering and business degrees from the University of Colorado resulted in many job interviews, including one with the CIA who liked my Jesuit training, along with my engineering degree. I received several job offers from major corporations like Westinghouse and General Motors who focused on my engineering degree.

I finally decided on a job with 3M Company, in their Instrument Department in Hawthorne, California. It was a small business within a large company, and it was in California. I was quite interested in getting out of Denver, which I viewed as a small town, and away from my domineering father and my distant mother. More importantly, I could use both my engineering and business degrees.

Jerry was the head of the Instrument Department. He was a real gentleman, who conceived of the idea of applying electronics to control chemical processes. He sold the idea to 3M's management, who chartered him to start a new business. Apparently he took a shine to me, as I enjoyed a very warm relationship with him and his wife Marge, including dinners at their home and sleeping on their sofa. Their daughter Mary Alice and I dated for a while.

Ed was the Instrument Department's sales manager. In addition to marketing literature, and though I had no training in sales techniques, Ed directed me to sell the Instrument Department's products around the Los Angeles area and in other States where there was no established sales representation.

3M acquired a company with a small computer. It became part of the Instrument Department. I sold a data logging system, based on this computer, to Northwest Natural Gas in Portland for use in keeping track of their widespread gas distribution system. I am grateful for this great experience, for a young man just out of college.

Somewhere along the way, my father talked to me about

clawing my way to the top of the corporate ladder. I see now that I did not understand his advice, in that I never focused on it. I just did my job, without reference to how others were maneuvering themselves. Later I was to learn a very hard lesson, about how hidden agendas entered into politics in organizations, even small ones.

I lived in apartments in Manhattan Beach and Hermosa Beach during my time with the Instrument Department. My most interesting living space was on the estate of Virginia Sinclair in the hills north of Santa Monica. Virginia was the heir to Sinclair Oil Company and a member of the Board of Directors of ARCO Oil. Virginia had built a small apartment on the grounds of her estate, for her son whose music was too loud for the house. I discovered this place from Mary Alice, who had lived there before me while she attended UCLA. Virginia took me to several interesting parties in Hollywood. I lived in this cottage on her estate until she fired her "house boy," and invited me to move into the big house in his place.

I moved into an apartment in Torrance. Two attractive women, Margie and Kate, whom I knew from college, moved into nearby cities. One was going to college in Long Beach, the other had a job in Camarillo. Each tried very hard to establish a relationship with me. While I enjoyed their company, I could not bring myself to settle down with either. I saw Margie after she moved back to Texas, when I traveled on business, but again no long-term connect.

Janet, one of the girls I knew from Loretto Heights College in Denver, lived in Palm Springs not far from her parents. Her father was a famous bandleader who had entertained the military at bases around the globe, and had established a rapport with some of the military brass. While visiting one weekend, we went to have dinner at her parents' home. Her father called me into his study. Cautious, I wondered what I had done wrong.

There he showed me a book that was labeled, *Top Secret Project Blue Book.* In that book was page after page of pictures of flying saucers. I was both startled and amazed. We talked about it for a while, but I failed to see the implications of what was before me. I went back to work on Monday and put it out of my mind, not mentioning what I had seen to anyone.

It was at the apartment in Torrance that I met my first wife, a very pretty blonde from Niagara Falls, New York. She was a stewardess for American Airlines. I fell in love almost immediately, and pursued her. It took me quite a long time to convince her to leave the airlines and marry me. In those days, her airline did not permit married stewardesses. Prior to being married, we had engaged in heavy petting, but no intercourse. She was terribly afraid of getting pregnant.

As soon as I met her family, my quiet inner voice spoke up. Her mother and father were extremely angry and judgmental, and her brother and sisters were not speaking to one other. Had I been listening, I would have walked away from the pending marriage ceremony; however, I was not conscious enough. On a positive note, if I had not married her, this world would have been deprived of two outstanding men: Kristopher and Kenton.

We were married in Niagara Falls, in a Catholic church, in the middle of a huge snowstorm. We got the last plane out for a couple of days, and hurried to Puerto Vallarta, Mexico, where we had a wonderful honeymoon. We moved into an apartment on the Esplanade in Redondo Beach, California. There we went about contented lives, enjoyed the beach, and each other.

At that time, I was attending a night program at the University of Southern California, where I was studying for my Master's in Business Administration. Once or twice a week, I commuted into central Los Angeles.

At the Instrument Department, we had an uphill battle convincing engineers responsible for chemical process to turn away from their traditional pneumatic controls. They did not trust the reliability of "these new fangled" electronic devices to control their complex chemical and petroleum processes. Against this resistance, the Instrument Department was not successful. It was closed down after a few years.

I was then transferred to the Mincom Division of 3M, where I sold drop-out compensators to the major television networks, ABC, CBS, and NBC. This device inserted analogue information into the electronic stream from video tape to smooth out any missing areas of magnetic material. This 3M division, headquartered in Camarillo, California, supplied large tape decks to unnamed government agencies.

Merle, my boss at Mincom, arranged for me to take a semester off to finish up my degree with full pay. I received my MBA degree from USC in 1966. This apparently put me high on some sort of a list for promotion, for I attracted the eye of Jack, the Marketing Manager for the Magnetic Products Division. At that time, Magnetic Products, the most profitable division in 3M Company, was headquartered at 3M corporate headquarters in Saint Paul, Minnesota.

My wife and I drove our Chevy convertible from seventy degrees in Southern California to minus thirty in Minnesota, a one hundred degree difference. A fact I heard about frequently. The city had run out of money to plow the street, so we drove in deep ruts, searching for an apartment.

Along with many others at 3M's corporate headquarters, I would idle our car at lunch time, to keep it warm enough to start after work in the below zero temperatures. During the winter months, at our apartment in St. Paul, I always remembered to plug in the block heater so that the car would start in the morning. My wife said that she had confused Minnesota and Mississippi, otherwise she would never have agreed to move to such a cold climate.

I worked in marketing research for Magnetic Products. Jack proved to be a very special mentor. 3M's magnetic tape technology was derived from what the Germans had used during World War II, to record Hitler's speeches. At the time I was there, 3M had a near monopoly in magnetic tape.

I did the research that led to 3M's introduction of magnetic recording cassettes. It was a major step for 3M, because the plastic case was as costly as was the tape inside. 3M's orientation had been to sell as many square yards of magnetic tape as possible. Division management eventually decided to join with Phillips of the Netherlands that was producing the cassette players.

During my time with Magnetic Products Division, I developed a stomach ulcer severe enough that I went to see a doctor. He prescribed milk and antacids. This condition persisted for several months. Following this, the ulnar nerve in both of my elbows became so severely inflamed that a doctor prescribed a cast for my left arm. This condition also eventually went away and has not bothered me since. During this same time, my wife wound up in the hospital with a severe case of hives from eating too many strawberries. As I look back at these from my current perspective, I see two people who were very insecure, shy, and fear-based. I recall that we were hesitant to venture out to go shopping at major department stores.

I ate lunch with a group of analysts from other Divisions of 3M. We became friendly to some extent, but not beyond work. Most of them boasted of MBA's from such schools as Harvard and Warton, and loved to downplay my lowly degree from USC.

Len worked for another division of 3M. He and I became friendly to the point that my wife and I were frequently invited to his parents' lake home north of Minneapolis. It was a pleasant experience and we felt like we had made some good friends.

I received a high draft number, but did not want to be drafted to be sent to Vietnam. 3M successfully petitioned to keep me in their employ, saying I had critical skills. This required legal action with a Minnesota high court.

I joined a Toastmasters group that met frequently in downtown St. Paul. This was my first exposure to speaking before a group. After a year, I was able to stand up and give a short presentation. Now, forty-five years later, I am an accomplished speaker, giving talks and workshops to audiences large and small, easily carrying on for over an hour, and channeling messages from non-human beings.

It was Jack's idea to attach a magnetic stripe to the back of credit cards. He saw the potential for using 3M's magnetic material, as a new way of capturing data. We worked on this for about a year, until he left 3M to go into private consulting.

It was not until Jack's departure that I thought about leaving 3M. He had been a great boss, someone who had seen something in an insecure young man and mentored him. Later I used Jack as a consultant at Columbine Venture Funds. I consider him to be a good friend who has supported my later explorations into the metaphysical, and with whom I still keep in touch.

I had proposed that the Magnetic Products Division acquire a small company in California that was developing the mechanisms for writing and reading magnetic stripe credit cards, American Computer and Communications. 3M management declined, saying that they wanted to focus on consumables, not hardware. Enthralled with the prospects for the magnetic stripped credit card, I investigated a job with AC&C.

My first son, Kristopher, was born in St. Paul. I recall how excited I was, and how disappointed that they would not allow me into the birth room, so I waited impatiently for word about my new child. With Kris' birth, and my new job at AC&C, we headed back for California, away from the snow and cold of Minnesota.

I found the culture of 3M Company to be one of genuinely caring about their employees, in addition to being very creative. As an example, they gave Jerry, the former head of the Instrument Department, a job in Minnesota after it closed down. I believe they were genuinely sorry to see me leave the company.

Back in California, my wife and I found a rental house in Palos Verdes, with a view overlooking the lights of greater Los Angeles. I loved the landscape, particularly the ice plant on the back hill and the large fuchsia bush next to the back door.

American Computers and Communications was in the initial stages of creating the electronic devices to record and read magnetic stripe credit cards. It was funded by two venture capitalists, Tommy Davis and Eugene Kliner, both with venture capital funds from the San Francisco area.

Tom, a seasoned manager, had been brought in to provide depth to the group of engineers who had founded the company. I worked as Vice President of Marketing.

I spent the next eighteen months convincing American Express, Bank of America, Master Card, and IATA (International Air Transport Association) to place a magnetic stripe on their credit cards. It was a slow process to change the way in which the banking system functioned.

AC&C created the readers for the original currency vending machines (now called ATMs) and for magnetic stripe readers at point-of-sale machines. The magnetic stripe credit card remained the standard for data capture from both credit and debit cards until the recent emergence of imbedded semiconductor chips.

This was an exciting time and I plunged into making a success of my work. A larger company, that dominated plastic credit cards, acquired AC&C. I left the company, because I did not like the management of the acquiring company. Tom stayed with AC&C, and eventually bought it back from the acquirer a few years later. He turned it into a success, selling to producers of ATMs and making data capture devices for banks.

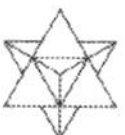

During my time in Minnesota, I had been introduced to the Institute for Executive Research headed by John Boyle. It was with John that I learned affirmations, about my "power factor," and other techniques for self-improvement. John taught me to relieve my anger, by working out on a heavy bag that I kept in our garage.

After I left AC&C, I went to work as a salesman for his Institute. My territory was Southern California. I soon learned that I could not sell what I had not internalized, and that my personality was not suited to knocking on the door of stockbrokers and other likely prospects. It was another learning experience. I was disappointed that I could not attune myself to something that was somewhat outside the mainstream of business. I left the Institute with no prospects of other employment, and with a severely damaged self-concept. Looking back on this, I see an experience that was necessary to my current status, as have been all my experiences. I do not see them as bad, only as learning opportunities.

At that time, we had a ranch style home on Oleander Street in Seal Beach that we bought for $39,000, and we had a mortgage. I felt under terrific pressure to return to earning a paycheck. My wife and I argued. As I recall, it was only the second time in my life that I got terribly angry, tipping over the dining room table.

After searching for months for a suitable job, while collecting unemployment checks, I landed a position at Motorola in Chicago. We did not want to move back to a cold climate, but I was desperate for a job. Motorola liked my 3M background, as they wanted to become more entrepreneurial. I convinced my wife that we were so desperate that we had no choice but to move.

We found a house in Lake Zurich, a short commute from Motorola's office in Des Plainse, Illinois. It was a split level on a large lot in a neighborhood of similar homes. Kristopher went to a nearby Montessori school.

Despite my aversion to heights, I painted the entire house a forest green with white trim. I found time to raise great quantities of vegetables in our back yard. We played bridge every Friday with neighbors. I played tennis on Saturday mornings. I drank beer and rum, joining with others in a weekend letdown and a hangover the next day. Life was reasonably relaxed and comfortable. I had a nice job. I had a happy family. I had friends in the neighborhood. The job allowed me to teach skiing at a local ski area, Fox Trails, at nights and on weekends.

My wife, son Kris, and I went on a cruise in the Caribbean. It was great fun visiting the various islands and eating meals several times each day on board. Everything went well until the captain turned into the path of Hurricane Alan off the coast of Haiti. For over a day, our huge cruise ship was battered by one hundred foot waves breaking over the bow. I still remember looking into the trough of those huge waves as the ship headed down into the next one. Everyone on board was sick, including the crew. There was a fire on board in the stabilizer room. At one point, all passengers were hustled to the boat deck. The crew seemed to think we might have to abandon ship. (In one hundred foot waves?) The ship limped back to Miami, where everyone scurried ashore.

At Motorola, I had landed in the New Ventures Department, where I was the lone businessperson charged with commercializing products dreamed up by a team of engineers under Ole. I investigated the market for electronic devices such as energy storage and electronic light bulbs. It was an interesting time of examining lots of new ideas.

I was imbedded in a 3rd Dimension culture of commercializing new technology based ideas. Unfortunately, none of the ideas that Ole's engineers came up with proved viable. After about two years, Motorola's New Ventures in Illinois was closed down.

I transferred to the Mergers and Acquisitions Office at Motorola's corporate headquarters under Keith. He was a young attorney, early forties, very full of himself, who Motorola management had recruited from their outside law firm, in order to get them into some new businesses. Under Keith, I was introduced to the world of investment banking, mergers, acquisitions, accounting, and law, all of which I found new and fascinating.

The offices of the Office of Mergers and Acquisitions were at O'Hare Plaza, right in the flight path to the airport. There was a health club next door at the Marriott Hotel, where Keith and I would work out regularly. I also played tennis doubles, with him and two executives from Motorola, at an indoor complex in Schaumberg.

When Motorola's new corporate office building was completed in Schaumberg, I was provided an office on the top floor. My 10 by 10 office had a door that was ten feet tall, matching the other doors on the floor. I climbed the twelve flights of stairs each morning as exercise for skiing. At that time I was driving a yellow Opel GT—not a great car for Illinois winters.

Keith loved to show his detailed knowledge of the law, wondering why I did not understand complex legal language. He became frustrated because I was unable to repeat, word for word, concepts I did not understand. I was treated as a very junior member of the team, being in my early thirties.

Soon after my arrival at Mergers and Acquisitions, Motorola divested its television business, and began to look for other opportunities. My job was strategic planning, wherein I wrote reports that envisioned new businesses for Motorola in cable television, broadcasting, digital communications, and satellites. I made several presentations to Bob Galvin, the Chairman of Motorola, who was quite open to new ideas. I interacted with Bill, Motorola's president, who provided a realistic note to some of our far flung proposals, and who wanted to keep Motorola focused on communications. Keith and I became closely allied with the Manager of Planning for the Communications Division, Jim, who wanted his division to diversify into digital, and with whom I played tennis once a week.

During this time, Motorola installed the world's first cell phone system in Chicago. The company stuck its toe into digital communications, after I had written a plan detailing the various opportunities in all facets of communications. I saw the workings of the world of acquisitions and mergers, as I rubbed shoulders with several of its high profile leaders. I traveled to Phoenix regularly, to interact with people in the semiconductor and government divisions. Usually I traveled by myself, and usually in the summer.

I was sent to the Motorola Executive Institute, in the Arizona desert, for a month. There I interacted with men who were being groomed for advancement within Motorola's various divisions. We had guest lectures almost every day, and were tested both psychologically and for skill levels. I was the youngest man there; my inferiority surfaced at their experience and aggressiveness, until I figured out that I was as smart as them, but that I lacked their desire to dominate. When I found out that I could play tennis as well as any of them, my self-confidence rose a bit. I may have been the youngest man present, but I was as good as them, at least in some ways.

My time at Motorola ended when I was offered the job to head up New Ventures. Thus far, it had not successfully launched any new businesses. What had started out as a promising new concept had failed, due to the rules established by Motorola's wage and salary administration. There was to be no special incentive compensation for managers of new enterprises, because it would conflict with positions in the established divisions of the company. I saw the handwriting on the wall, but said that I would undertake the job if I got some sort of incentive compensation. I was told that I was not high enough in the organization to qualify, so I made plans to leave Motorola.

A few months after I had departed from Motorola, I got crosswise with Keith Bane, because Keith and I had interacted with a business broker from Seattle who had brought an acquisition to Motorola, that Motorola had ultimately done. I felt sure that he had been promised a commission; Keith refused to admit it. I was deposed by Motorola's attorney. Keith promised me that if I testified in court that he would "come after me with the legal resources of a major corporation." Fearing a costly legal battle, I subsequently declined to appear in court.

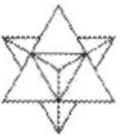

It was time to move back to Denver, so I began to search. I felt that I had achieved enough self-confidence that I now could be in the same town with my mother and father. I found an opportunity with National City Lines, where I would pursue acquisitions and investments on behalf of this NYSE corporation.

The three of us moved into a newly built home in Aurora, far across town from my parent's house. It had a great view of the mountains of Colorado's Front Range. We furnished it with what we had brought from Illinois. I hauled many loads of gravel for landscaping, planted junipers and small trees, and placed sod for grass front and back.

Prior to my move back to Denver, Grandma Bee had died. I attended her funeral, but missed the chance to say goodbye to her in her last days. Not long after we moved back, Gramps was taken to the hospital. He had suffered a heart attack while mowing the grass in his back yard. I did visit him in the hospital, and had the opportunity to connect with him before he passed over. I was very sad at the passing of these two, who had meant so much to me during my growing up years. When I attempt to connect with them these days, energies of love and acceptance come over me, and they encourage me to continue on my path. I am very grateful for the love they supplied during my formative years.

National City Lines was headquartered in the Denver Tech Center just off I-25. At that time NCL had a number of operating subsidiaries in trucking and transportation, including the bus system in Houston and the toll bridge across the Rio Grande at El Paso, and a Denver-based trucking company.

Originally the company had been created by General Motors, as a way to sell its busses. NCL would finance and operate a bus system for a city, if the city would tear up its existing street car tracks. At one time NCL had many cities under contract, including Denver.

NCL was run by a most interesting man, Skip Pratt. I was immediately put on the Boards of several NCL subsidiaries. Mr. Pratt told me, "I'll tell you how to vote."

Skip Pratt would come into the office each morning about eight. He would take care of business until eleven thirty, when he would head home for lunch with his wife, and watch his favorite soap-opera on TV. In the afternoons, he went to Cherry Hills Country Club, to play gin rummy.

I was charged with finding new businesses. Mr. Pratt liked to buy small positions, in public companies, on the open market, being careful to stay below the percentage ownership when it became necessary to report this activity to the SEC. Mr. Pratt and I parted company when he asked me to put a hundred thousand of my own money into the deals I was proposing, money that I did not have.

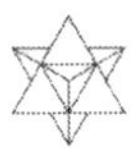

I had watched the venture capitalists who had funded AC&C, and knew that I wanted to be one of them. It was an ideal job. Placing a little money in a business, and then showing up once a month for a board of directors meeting. So I set out to start a venture fund in Denver. I soon encountered Keith, who had both money and connections within the local business community. He was interested in what I was proposing, and offered both money and stock in one of his companies to seed the venture. We founded ENERVEST, Inc., as a Small Business Investment Company, so we could obtain low cost loans from the government, with which to fund businesses.

In a humble office in Denver, we began to search out opportunities. It soon became obvious that my orientation was towards high tech, whereas Keith wanted to look at everything. It also became apparent that Keith was not constrained by certain accepted business practices.

For the first time I faced the pressure of meeting payroll, both for myself and for a secretary, then later for a young associate. It was a major life change from accepting a paycheck from a corporation, and much more intensive than starting a new job. I assembled a good Board of Directors, made up of investors in ENERVEST; they acted as a rein on some of Keith's more outlandish ideas.

Despite this, I made time to interact with my young son, Kristopher, as he joined Indian Guides and I, briefly, coached his soccer team. We spent hours throwing balls in the back yard of our home, learning to ride his bicycle, and showing him how to fly fish. Kris and I went skiing, fairly often; later he became quite an accomplished skier, as a member of USC's ski team.

At the same time, I enjoyed the company of others in the venture capital business. I was a member of the Board of the National Association of Small Business Investment Companies. Our annual meetings ranged from the Broadmoor in Colorado Springs to the island of Bermuda. These were lavish affairs, with banquets and golf. In addition to enjoying events like these, my wife and I vacationed in Europe and Mexico. We fished on the Kimmel family property in the mountains west of Denver, and skied during the winters.

My relationship with my wife suffered, as I spent more time at ENERVEST. We argued frequently, primarily about her approach to disciplining Kristopher. She was angry much of the time.

Following an old pattern, I sent Kristopher off to Regis High School, something for which he has never forgiven me. This involved a long bus ride, until he was old enough to drive. This whole picture, coupled with my later divorce of his mother, caused conflict with Kris, that both he and I have gone to great efforts to repair in subsequent years.

From 1978 until 1983, ENERVEST funded twenty businesses, ranging from a coal mine in Paonia, Colorado, to high technology companies in Boulder. It was a portfolio that resulted in several bankruptcies, a few "living dead," and one stellar success.

ENERVEST supplied the first $25,000 to two young men in Boulder, who wanted to develop a means of measuring blood oxygen non-invasively. After several infusions of capital, BIOX had a working prototype. (In a doctor's office or hospital, an oximeter is clipped on your finger and measures oxygen saturation.)

After a couple of years, Keith wanted to sell the technology and reap an immediate profit. I was determined to stay the course until we had a real product. It went for a shareholders vote. After a tumultuous meeting, during which several members of the Board of Directors threatened to resign, Keith's family, who owned a majority of the stock of ENERVEST, decided things my way.

BIOX went on to develop its product. The company was eventually sold to British Oxygen with Keith and his family making several million. The two inventors made about ten million dollars each, and I made over $1.5 million. ENERVEST was generally recognized as a huge success, returning over 45% compounded to its investors. The PULSE OXIMETER has become a standard of care throughout the world.

My second son, Kenton, was born in Denver in December of 1991. My wife did not want another child. This caused further turmoil in our relationship.

I still recall vividly, Kenton's birth and how I got to hold him moments later. That provided a bond of love with him that has surpassed all of the turmoil of my divorce from his mother, her continuing anger at me since the divorce, and the fact that she took Kenton to California despite my objections.

During this time, my wife and I became involved with a group called "Creative Initiative." (They were later to be known as "Beyond War.") There I found a group of highly conscious individuals who were interested in personal evolution, as a means of making the world a peaceful place. They saw things in terms of people helping each other, and taking responsibility for the environment. It was quite different from my venture capitalist point of view. Since they frowned on alcohol, I gave up drinking alcohol for a period of two years—a very important milestone for me. I recall being in a large audience in Denver, as a Creative Initiative program was being broadcast from Palo Alto, California. One of the messages was that capitalism was not the answer to the world's problems.

Creative Initiative required the participation of both married people. My wife did not want to continue with them, saying they were not much fun. So we were forced to drop out. Yet, I had become committed to a way of thinking that took me out of my self-centered cocoon, and showed me a path to further maturity. Creative Initiative was a factor that led to the breakup of our marriage.

I went back to a Regis High School reunion. There I found that both of my closest friends from high school, Dennis and Jerry, had divorced and remarried. This opened my eyes to this possibility. Up to that time, I had assumed that I was stuck in my unhappy marriage according to strict Catholic dogma, and my family's adherence to it.

Soon after that event, I came to recognize that my relationship with my wife had deteriorated to where I felt that my health was threatened. I went to a doctor. He saw something on his EKG and referred me to a specialist. I had several non-invasive tests, including a sonogram. I wore a Holter Monitor for a few days. After a treadmill test, with a cardiologist, he diagnosed me with an irregular heartbeat. He told me to stop drinking coffee and Coke.

My wife and I were not communicating, my job was very intense, and I could not come home to peace and quiet. Angry at not being able to better the situation, I asked for a divorce and moved out of the house. This impacted Kristopher particularly, a teenager who did not want his parents to separate; he blamed me totally.

Our divorce dragged on for eighteen months, because my wife was convinced that I had squirreled away millions of dollars in Switzerland. When BIOX was sold, I had received $1.5 million. She and her attorney had their eyes on the cash. I hustled my accountant to prepare my tax return and wrote a check for over five hundred thousand to the IRS before I went into court. This burst her attorney's strategy to stick me with a large tax bill. We were then able to negotiate a settlement, wherein I supplied my soon-to-be ex-wife with enough cash that she did not need to work, so she could be a stay-at-home mother with Kenton and remain in our house in Aurora.

Within a year of our divorce, my now former wife moved to California, taking Kenton with her. She wanted to be close to Kris, who was enrolled at the University of Southern California. I fought the move with an attorney, but ultimately was powerless to stop her moving out of Colorado. I had a ten-year contract with Columbine Venture Fund, and needed to provide support payments.

I visited Kris,whenever we could arrange his schedule in Los Angeles with mine in Orange County, where Kenton lived. I was somewhat reluctant to visit Kris very often, as he always repeated his mother's assertions that I should abandon my business in Colorado and move to California, so I could be close to Kenton. She made Kris the man of the household fathering Kenton.

I arranged my board meetings so I could be in Southern California, visiting with Kenton one or two weekends each month, plus holidays and summer vacations. We enjoyed our time together, but it was all too brief. The hardest thing I have ever had to do was to drop Kenton off at his mother's house, at the end of a visit. Each time, I felt as if I had been stabbed in the heart. This was all wrong. It wasn't meant to be this way. Somehow I had failed my son. My whole body sunk into the seat of the automobile. My breathing became irregular. As I drove away, I was barely able to concentrate on the road. Even as I boarded the airplane, the feelings did not leave me. It was a sense of failure and helplessness.

I regret the turmoil I caused in the lives of both Kristopher and Kenton. Both have grown into mature and successful individuals. Both are very good fathers to their children. I now have five grandchildren, whom I visit as often as possible. I retain bragging rights, for both of my sons in their business ventures. I regret that my former wife is still angry at me.

The divorce proved to be pivotal because my father and mother disowned me. I was no longer invited to holiday celebrations like Thanksgiving, Christmas and Easter. My siblings fell in line with our parents. It was a time of great emotional turmoil and loneliness, both from the effects of the divorce, and from my family's rejection.

My father died without reconciling with me; I did visit him in the hospital and said thanks for everything. I had my job, but not much else.

Eventually, after my mother lost one eye to cancer, she allowed me back into her life, albeit rather tentatively. I did hug her when she was in home hospice, and felt a connection. My mother may have suspected that something changed in me when I came into my body, but she never discussed it with me.

It was only after I married Heidi that my family began to welcome me back. By that time my father had died. My mother came to my wedding with Heidi, but my younger brother Brian did not.

I have since communicated with both my mother and father telepathically. My mother asks me only to understand that she was very young when she gave birth to me. She asks me to understand that she was very young when she had me, and did her best, including following the advice of others. As to why we never connected later on, she says that she saw the change in me when I walked in, and did not understand it within the framework of the Catholic religion. My father and I dwell on the good things he was able to do for me. I express my gratitude for them. He expresses regrets for his judgments about me and harsh treatment. I am sure that, now, both parents understand why I was so different from the rest of their kids.

I entered a period of intense personal growth. I learned to function on my own. More importantly, I totally severed all connection to the Catholic religion. While I retained some guilt from the divorce, I set out to find new ways to live.

I had relationships with a number of women. I had two marriages of about a year each. I will always be grateful to the wonderful women from these years. They softened a hard-nosed businessman, made me less self-centered, and assisted my growth toward the path to which I am now firmly committed. I would not be where I am today without their assistance.

These thirteen years of turmoil produced important changes in me. I softened my approach to many things, including my behavior toward women in general, no longer seeing them as objects or possessions. I began to listen to my quiet inner voice. I opened myself to explore and accept new concepts. However, I was still cocooned within the conventional paradigm of anger, drama, judgment, irritability, and feelings of less than. My receipt of a large payment, as the result of ENERVEST's investment in BIOX lessened my insecurity, so that I was set up to pursue my next chapter in the venture capital business.

At the same time, events and changes were taking place in my private life, I formed Columbine Ventures with four partners, raising $35 million in funds, from sources like the pension funds of Exxon and Ford, Mellon Bank, insurance companies, Japanese investors, a corporation in Europe, and wealthy individuals. Our charter was to invest in small companies, and receive a ten-fold return within five years. My partners were Sherman, who had been with me at ENERVEST, David, who ran a local computer company, Duane, who had invented the smoke detector, and Terry, who had been with Diamond Shamrock ventures. We rented offices in a new building, overlooking I-25 in the Denver Tech Center.

I was extremely busy with everything that was happening. My shoulders became stiff and my neck muscles cramped up. At times, I had to wear a neck brace just to get through the day. Then I met a massage therapist, Susan, at a party. She immediately recognized the tight muscles in my neck, barely touching them was painful. After a few sessions with her, I was a new person. I have valued massage ever since, and have learned about the spiritual relationship that some practioners have with the bodies upon which they work.

At that same time, my hearing loss became more evident to me. I expect it had been increasing since my childhood bouts with severe colds and nose drops. I find myself busy lip-reading, unable to look in the eyes of others, as I struggle to catch their words. It is especially acute in large groups, or situations with lots of background noise. This condition has persisted to this day, and makes it difficult for me to enjoy groups, movies, or lectures. It also causes me to be shy, in situations other than quiet conversation with small groups. This explains why I am a writer and enjoy speaking to large groups.

At Columbine, we invested in fifty companies, mainly early stage start-ups, in everything from semiconductors, to semiconductor processing equipment, to computer software, to medical devices, to biotechnology. These investments were in companies located from San Diego to Boston. After a couple of years, the partnership seemed to be working okay, and we set out to raise a second fund. We did raise a second fund of forty-four million dollars.

At that time, I was on an advisory board of the U.S. operations of Great Life Insurance. We would meet once a quarter to review the latest analysis of their in-house economists. Once a year we went for a retreat to some place like Acapulco, Mexico. I was also on the Small Business Council for the State of Colorado. It was headed by Roy Romer, State Treasurer. Romer later became Governor of Colorado. I was also involved in creating the Boulder Business Incubator for commercializing and mentoring new high technology businesses.

About that time, David Miller developed a conflict of interest between Columbine and his own businesses. I was vacationing in China when the other partners informed me that they had decided he had to leave the partnership, for the good of all. At the time, I was not aware of the intrigue that was developing among the other partners, as I was too involved in my personal life. So I agreed to their wisdom in the matter.

Not long after, we hired a replacement for David, Carl, a business acquaintance of Terry. I did not see where this might lead, as Terry sought to enhance his status within the partnership.

We did go on to raise an additional fund, ultimately finding ourselves with about $80 million under management. As promised to our investors, we invested in electronics, software, medical devices, and biotechnology, with each partner specializing in one area. Over the course of a year, each partner read hundreds of business plans, visited many potential investments, and selected one or two to present to the other partners for ratification.

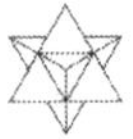

In late 1987 and early 1988, I had two incidents that changed my life. In the first one, I was reclining on my bed in broad daylight, when suddenly high intensity energy, not unlike something electric, entered my body through the top of my shoulders. It was powerful enough to lift me a foot off the bed. After catching my breath, I dismissed it entirely, but have never forgotten it.

The second occurred weeks later, when at bedtime, I felt very powerful energies at the foot of my bed. I saw nothing, only felt their powerful energies. Frightened, I demanded that they go away. This occurred several nights in a row. I dismissed it, and went back to work, back to the conventional paradigm.

I now understand that these two events were my wake-up calls, to begin the life for which I, as a soul, had come into this body. Several years later, I underwent hypnotic regression, wherein I experienced myself floating above my bed as my physical body trembled at the presence of three powerful beings.

At about this same time, I was presented with a copy of the Urantia Book. It made an immediate impression on me, for it contained information on the universe, wrapped in somewhat familiar information about God. I devoured the two thousand page Book, cutting it into small sections with a razor, so I could take them on my business trips. I had another Urantia Book rebound into three smaller books. For the first time, I believed in the reality of beings on other planets. I attended weekly meetings of a study group, headquartered in Boulder.

Only after I had seen my first UFO, and had benefitted from channeled information, did I see the limitations of the material in the Urantia Book. There was no mention of the proximity of extraterrestrials. There was nothing about reincarnation. Little did I see then that the Urantia Book was an important step to my involvement with extraterrestrials, and my personal evolution. It was also the way in which I finally unplugged from my attachment to seeing things as a Catholic. The same can be said for books like the Bible, for in them there is no mention of extraterrestrials or reincarnation.

My Columbine business partners noticed a change in me almost immediately. "You're different," one said. I replied that I liked who I was. "You're no longer the eagle with the blood on its beak," another commented. Again, I insisted that I liked the new me, and continued with business as usual.

In the following months, I saw myself increasingly disagreeing with the other four, first about little things, then important issues. It took a while, along with turmoil in my personal life, but they eventually confronted me with the ultimatum that I was no longer welcome in the partnership.

It was a severe blow for me to contemplate leaving something I had founded; I looked upon myself as the leader of the other partners. I felt betrayed by the men whom I had pulled together to create Columbine. Under the terms of the partnership, we were all equal partners; a mistake I had made at the onset.

After a final confrontation with them, I accepted a generous severance package, and went to look for other opportunities. Columbine Venture Funds did not perform to the expectations of its investors; it failed to return their initial investment.

Looking back at that event, I am most grateful that it moved me away from my attachment to the world of business and making money, so that I could begin the mission for which I came to Earth. I should have been happy to turn my back on the venture capital business: traveling almost every week to a board meeting somewhere; arguing for an investment I wanted to make with partners who did not understand either the technology or market; constantly being aware of my obligations to the investors who had risked their funds with Columbine.

However, my bruised ego did not see things that way. What I did not see at the time was that this turn of events opened the way for me to move out of the cocoon of the conventional paradigm. Blaming others, I was reluctant to admit my lack of focus on business. Until I completely left the business world, I did not see that what had happened to me in 1988 had caused me to re-focus my life.

My departure from Columbine dredged up all my old feelings of less-than and unworthiness. I was angry at my former partners. I was lost with what was to happen next.

Looking back at the situation, I see that I acquired a valuable experience to help others who have lost a job. I can relate to their feeling, as they look back and look forward. I felt the judgment of many others after I left Columbine; I can also relate that to other people.

Taking a break, Kristopher and I went to Canada on a guided fishing trip. We took horses into the back country north of Edmonton. It was cloudy and rainy. Most of what we caught were mushrooms. Later, fly fishing, we floated the Elb River near Calgary. It was my attempt to connect with him. All in all, we had a great time together. Nonetheless, he remained critical of my action with regard to Kenton and his mother.

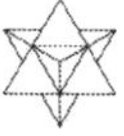

For the next five years, I bounced around various business opportunities. I found three experienced businessmen, Chet, Frank, and Paul, and formed Paradigm Partners. We had a small office on Walnut Street in Boulder. After my Columbine experience, I was very happy to find men who would join with me in a business adventure. We briefly ran the Boulder Technology Incubator. I explored the idea of establishing an institute, centered around holistic health.

Paradigm Partners explored the leveraged buyout business.

Chet, Frank, and I came very close to consummating a deal in the specialty coatings business with a $50 million loan commitment from Chase Bank. When Chemical Bank acquired Chase, the deal did not suit them. We scurried around, and with the help of men from the former Chase Bank, we secured a loan commitment from Bank of America, but by then the seller had found another purchaser; the deal fell apart.

We looked at starting anew for another opportunity, but looking at my personal bank account, I saw that I had invested more than $200,000 in finding a suitable business opportunity. I was tempted to continue. However, something within me said, "No more." I listened to my inner voice and told my business partners that I simply was not prepared to go further.

One indication of my mindset at that time was an incident in New York. Our friends at Chase Bank had set me up to attend a large presentation by a highly respected guru in the leverage buy-out arena. I joined a room filled with two hundred men in dark suits. When the cigars were passed around, I knew I did not belong there, and began to sweat. This is a condition that had plagued me, whenever I found myself in circumstances where I felt I was not comfortable, like making a presentation before the Independent Bankers of Colorado, to explain venture capital when the speaker just before me had already given my speech. At the meeting in New York, my white dress shirt became dripping wet. I excused myself from the table and fled to the men's room, where I found my shorts were also wet with perspiration. When I returned to the table, there was cognac being passed around. The man next to me asked if I was okay. I replied that I was fine. After the presentation, I quickly left, saying to myself, "I know I don't belong with these people."

Not long after this incident, in the summer of 1996, I resigned from any lingering Boards of Directors, any involvement with small businesses, and stopped reading business plans.

In Summary:

I am sharing this summary of my life as a businessman and father, because what I will present in subsequent chapters is so far removed from this period of my life. I hope that you will see me, as I was then, as a human being trapped in the cocoon of the conventional paradigm.

I can see three benefits from my thirty-three years in the business world. First, involvement with wealthy and powerful people, to see how the conventional paradigm benefits them. Second, achieving some measure of success, in order to advance me beyond a shy, introverted man. Third, interacting with a number of women, who smoothed my hard exterior and brought forth a more sensitive man. Fourth, accumulating enough money to allow me to follow my path, although those funds have now been largely exhausted.

I lived quite well during the later years of my business life, when I was a venture capitalist. I overcame a very low self-concept, depression, severe acne, stomach ulcers, and an attraction to alcohol. However, my hearing loss has remained with me.

During my thirty-three years in business, I lived on the cutting edge of new technologies, receiving information from a whole variety of sources. I provided money and mentoring to over seventy companies, mostly high technology. I am now living on the cutting edge of information, about a larger reality, that far surpasses anything of the technology or lifestyle of the conventional paradigm.

Looking back at those years, I now see that I was not in touch with who I really was beyond becoming a successful businessman, and living in the cocoon prescribed by the conventional paradigm.

In my business years, I had cycled between fear, depression, self-centeredness, anger, and inadequacy, to determination, self-reliance, elation, happiness, and pride. I had only my traditional religious beliefs to fall back on. These proved inadequate. I studied the Urantia Book, clinging to its revelations about the universe and God. I explored alternate religious beliefs, such as Unity and

Religious Science. I did maintain my core belief in God and a moral center based on traditional values. I used workshops to foster my business career. However, at the end of this period, I had no clear meaning for my life.

If I had continued with that lifestyle, I saw my own future, and the future of my world, as extrapolations of what I knew at that moment. I turned my back on all this. Many would call it a crazy decision. Yet, I somehow knew that it was important to succeed in my former lifestyle, and then turn my back on it to demonstrate the one hundred eighty decision that I made.

I recall one evening, after I was no longer associated with Columbine Venture Funds, after I had no close family, and after I had no permanent residence, when I gave up. I said to God, "All right, I've tried it my way, and look where it's gotten me. I give up. From now on, I am going to do it your way."

As you will see in the following chapters, my transformation from businessman to who I now am, exposes a path for anyone struggling to achieve higher consciousness. I am testimony to the reality that it can be done. Did I receive extraordinary help? Yes, but keep in mind, I am a wayshower blazing a path out of 3rd and 4th Dimensions. The fact that I made my transformation opens the door to a much easier path for others to follow, for you to follow.

PART II

Larger Picture

3

This Part II is about my awakening to the Larger Picture, as I became aware of the reality of extraterrestrials. Looking back at this juncture, I see just how radical a change I made in my first years away from the business world. My attitude about religion, politics, money, health care, conflict, relationships, and my self-concept all experienced one-hundred eighty degree turns.

Moving forward seventeen years, I now see the things very differently, once more, than I did when I was first exposed to extraterrestrials. At that later moment, my Larger Picture expanded even further, as I began communicating with extraterrestrials, and publishing observations about Earth and humanity from their point-of-view.

Although I did not realize it at the time, my adoption of an unconventional life took a major step forward when I met Heidi, in the spring of 1996. She had met me at a costume Valentine's Day party a month earlier. We were attending a divorce recovery and relationship improvement class, under the guidance of Will, in Boulder, Colorado. She and I went on to assist Will with future classes for the next nine months.

Heidi and I were married in September of 1999. Since we became a couple, she has been a wonderful companion and supporter for my incredible journey with extraterrestrials and non-physicals. We both function at much higher levels of consciousness, than either thought possible when we first met. Her background in health has kept us functioning in good health, well past the age when the bodies of others have failed them. At our current home in California, we enjoy the beach as often as possible, play pickleball several times per week, visit the families of my two sons with five grandchildren, and enjoy the congeniality of the 4th Dimension people in our neighborhood.

Heidi and I have now been together for over twenty years. I am most grateful that she and I have managed to stick it out through a couple of rough moments. I appreciate her insights and intuition. She has been a constant supporter, as I have followed my unconventional path. I love her very much.

After finishing that first course with Will, I took a week off to hike the Colorado Trail with my nephew, Travis, and sister-in-law, Deb. We used llamas, to enable us to hike many miles at elevations over twelve thousand feet. The scenic views along the way were fantastic: rugged mountains, endless forests, clear streams, and many wildflowers.

I stayed in touch with Heidi by phone. She and I had our first date at a Colorado Rockies baseball game in June. We dated exclusively from that point on and fell in love. Our connection remains strong today. She has been involved in my adventures with extraterrestrials and our climb to higher consciousness. She remains my most valued supporter.

As we begin this Part II, let me acknowledge that there is, often times, caution and/or ridicule around the whole subject of extraterrestrials. I believe this is due to four factors: 1) This arena is indeed new and strange to many people. It is more difficult to accept the presence of these non-humans on our planet than it is the existence of angels, or the reality of strange beings, but in some distant star system. 2) The media, books, and movies, especially in the United

States, portray the subject as something weird, crazy, fearful, and/or merely science fiction. 3) The vast majority of extraterrestrials in the universe are benevolent, friendly; they function at a higher frequency than most humans and with a higher consciousness. This makes it difficult for those of higher vibration to appear in physical form in our lower vibration. 4) There are detrimental (dark) ETs present on Earth who have been engaged in dominating humanity for a long time, and for a variety of reasons. They operate at frequencies in which they can manifest in physical forms. To provide frames of reference, I will elaborate on all four of these points as we go along with my story of contact with extraterrestrials, and how it raised my consciousness beyond the conventional paradigm.

During the summer of 1996, my son, Kenton, and I went to England where we stayed in a country house outside London, and rode bicycles to get to the grocery store. It required a lot of creative energy to come up with acceptable meals from the basic larder I found in the rental. It was even more challenging to play gin rummy with Kenton, who has an almost total recall of the cards that showed up.

From England, we went to Switzerland, taking the train to Jungfrau and exploring Zurich. It was an important time for the two of us to connect, since I had been seeing him only on weekends and during his vacations. It was a time I will long remember, for camaraderie and love, and my feelings of doing something really worthwhile.

It was at about this time that I was walking in the "B" concourse at Denver International Airport, stretching my legs prior to a flight. Suddenly, I was pushed to one side by an invisible force. It was so powerful that I stumbled into a chair to prevent myself from falling on the floor. A voice in my head said something like this, "We would like to introduce you to some very important people." I responded, still not awake to what was really going on, "Okay, but I'm going to need some new clothes and money, so I can travel." They said, "Not to worry, we will take care of all that." It took me quite some time before I was able to stand and walk to my flight.

This was my first telepathic contact, and to say the least, the words were crude, as was my reaction to them. Looking back at it, I see how I was completely misunderstanding an invitation to connect with my extraterrestrial friends. I was still functioning from my businessman viewpoint. This included my translation of the word "people," rather than the word "beings."

Heidi and I were living in Boulder. I had quit the venture capital business and was looking at what came next. I felt I wanted something very different, something disconnected from the business world. After many conversations, primarily with non-business types, including ex-Governor Richard Lamm, I decided to go back to school to get a Master's Degree in Psychology. Something told me that I needed to look at things from a new perspective. At the same time, I had no idea how I might spend the next twenty or fifty years of my life. I just had a strong feeling that I needed to do something very different from my business career.

That summer and the following year, Heidi and I climbed several fourteen-thousand foot peaks in Colorado, the "fourteeners." As members of the Colorado Mountain Club, we went on hikes every week. In the following winter, we snowshoed into Brainard Lake and stayed overnight at the Mountain Club's cabin. I bicycled several times a week on the roads east of Boulder.

That fall, I enrolled for my psychology degree at Regis College in Denver because the course was self-directed and allowed maximum flexibility. I am grateful to both my faculty advisor, James, and my overseer, Paul, for the latitude and advice they provided me during my course of studies. The course work was loosely structured, which gave me ample opportunity for self-examination. At this early stage of my course work, I did not yet see myself in terms of being a chrysalis in a cocoon of the conventional paradigm, a cocoon into which I had been trained by the beliefs of others. Rather I focused on absorbing the conventional theories of psychology, studying the assigned material, and writing academic papers.

One of the most memorable aspects of my participation in the Regis program was my time with the Woman's Shelter in Boulder. During their training classes to sensitize participants in the plight of battered women, I came face to face with aspects of life I had dismissed during my career as a businessman. I visited the secret location of the Shelter, where women and their children had sought refuge. I also learned that many of them, out of a sense of low self-worth, returned to the violent situation from which they had fled. I rode with a Boulder County Sheriff as he responded to a call for help. In these moments, I saw, first hand, the worst of the conventional paradigm: fear, insecurity, judgment, polarization, and drama. And I saw my reaction to it, as I examined my own feelings.

I feel my time with the Safe House was a necessary step in my climb to higher consciousness, enabling me to move from my privileged point of view, as a successful venture capitalist, to one embracing new facets of humanity, particularly those I had formerly dismissed as below me. I recall agonizing during the lectures at the Safe House, as I saw my former lifestyle crumble in light of new information about the plight of the less fortunate. I became ashamed with my earlier blind side, and resolved to henceforth see others as my brothers and sisters. I now see this training was key to helping me completely turn my back on the conventional paradigm.

My course work at Regis allowed many opportunities for self-examination. I wrote paper after paper about how I had behaved in the past, how I had treated other people without caring, and how my drive to become a successful businessman had driven all of my actions. These courses prepared me to counsel with clients about the very things I found in myself. It also prepared me to listen to others as they struggle with their issues inside the conventional paradigm.

My internship was group work with teenagers, who had been court-mandated for counseling, an experience far removed from my days as a venture capitalist. I was one of three interns. Out of six kids in the program, we were able to help only one re-unite with his parents. This moved me to understand not only mental health, but to have empathy for kids trapped in cocoons dictated by parents, for we also worked with the kid's parents, during this program.

Looking back on my degree in psychology, I see I was taught theories and practices to help people cope within the conventional paradigm. Neither the larger picture or love were ever put forth as ways to influence problems of the psyche. There was no discussion about higher consciousness as a way to move away from the fear, drama, polarity, and other attributes of the conventional paradigm. Nonetheless, pursuing this degree was extremely valuable for me, in that it enabled me to move away from my self-concept, as a successful businessman who enjoyed the finer things of life.

My first book, *Trillion*, spilled out of my computer in September of 1997. At the time, I was working on an academic paper for my degree. I had thoughts about an institute and believed writing them down might help. What resulted was far removed from that initial thought.

I wasn't quite sure what was going on, as I had no intention of writing a book. I now know that the book was helped along by a process known as "automatic writing," and that it was the result of higher consciousness. Previously, I had written advertising copy, legal documents, business plans and academic papers. A book, particularly a book in story form, was well beyond my intention and abilities. At the same time, a book with a fictional background enabled me to comfortably relay what I knew about the Larger Picture.

So, here it was, a story about a group of extraterrestrials who were living in the Arizona desert, seeking to help humanity. At first I believed I was writing a science fiction story. Then I began to see the deeper meanings woven into the book. I did not acknowledge the assistance I was receiving; later I welcomed it.

In about ninety days, I had a story and characters. I continued working toward my psychology degree, as I took a creative writing class at the University of Colorado in Boulder.

While all of this was going on, I found time to go hiking with our dog, Amber, every day. We lived near the Flatirons, rock formations jutting upward from the foothills west of Boulder. The trail along these red rocks was the hike Amber and I covered almost each day. Another hike was to the top of Mount Sanitis, near Boulder, a fifteen hundred foot climb. With Heidi and Amber, I enjoyed hiking to Boulder Creek, in the mountains west of Boulder, where we found an idyllic trout stream with few other fishermen.

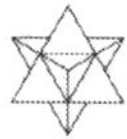

In the summer of 1998, I journeyed to Adelaide, Australia to study Narrative Therapy under Michael White, its originator. Narrative Therapy is about rewriting one's story, in order to rewrite one's life. It was taught in many universities and had proven to be very effective in treating many psychological problems.

After ten days with Michael, he informed me that he could see that my real passion was the book I was writing, rather than becoming a psychotherapist. Although I was reluctant to give up on something I had spent almost two years pursing, I had to agree.

Heidi, Kenton, and Kris met me in Sidney, Australia. In an attempt to help with jet lag, I took them from the airport to the Sidney Opera House, where the three immediately fell asleep. The second day, we found the zoo where Kenton petted a Koala bear and we saw a Tasmanian devil. Kris went off to scuba dive on the Great Barrier Reef, while Kenton, Heidi and I went to Fitzroy Island on the northeast coast for a few days of relaxing.

Journeying to New Zealand, we four tried skiing on the South Island, but the snow was not there. Then Kenton, Heidi, and I rode the train, from the southern tip of the South Island to Auckland on the North Island. Along the way, we enjoyed green-lipped mussels at every opportunity. We stopped in Picton, while they loaded the train onto ferries, and had the best fish and chips ever. A couple of days later, Kenton and Heidi went swimming with the dolphins in the ocean off the North Island.

Returning home to Ridgway, Colorado, where Heidi had a new teaching job, I bought software to help me understand plot, character development, and suspense. *Trillion* underwent several rewrites as I struggled to express myself. Not yet ready to admit that I was getting outside help, I wrote in a world of what I believed was my imagination. At the same time, a feeling of accepting my new role as an author overcame me. Surprisingly, I had little fear or anxiety of what lay ahead for us, and little judgment of those who questioned what I was doing, rather than getting a real job.

I attended a writer's workshop on the Gulf shore of Alabama. I learned that my writing was "quite good," and that my manuscript was coming along. One of the participants wanted to make a movie based on it, particularly after he learned that I had been in the venture capital business and possibly had access to funding.

I hired two experienced editors out of New York. The first chopped up my manuscript so thoroughly that I spent a year rewriting it. The second did a line edit, and contributed much to my writing style. However, she told me I would never get my book published in New York, because it lacked the requisite sex and violence, and talked about extraterrestrials. Having helped to start and nurture over seventy new businesses in my career as a venture capitalist, I set about starting my own publishing company, *Paradigm Books*.

At that time I did not understand the dynamics of the alternative publishing business. I had my sights set on a bestseller. Later, I came to realize that my market was limited to the niche of those who had an interest in extraterrestrials. The market for my books has now become those who wish to know about higher consciousness, and how they can contribute to the resurrection of Earth—an even smaller market niche.

Regis allowed me to use the manuscript for *Trillion* as my Master's thesis. I subsequently graduated in 2000 with a Degree in Psychology. I have never practiced as a psychotherapist, although I am good at listening to people's issues, and very good at reading energies. I enjoy participating in small group discussions, particularly those of higher consciousness.

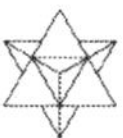

In the fall of 2000, Heidi and I journeyed to Roswell, New Mexico. After prowling around the International UFO Museum and Research Center, I felt that indeed something had transpired there in 1947. I was particularly impressed by the numerous written accounts of people involved in the incident. This sparked a memory of my father showing me an article out of a Denver newspaper about the crash of a UFO in New Mexico. I quickly discovered that the human-like extraterrestrials in *Trillion* were nothing like the ones who had crashed their ship in Roswell.

On April 9, 2001, The Center For The Study of Extraterrestrial Intelligence (CSETI), headed by Dr. Steven Greer, presented the Disclosure Project. On a live Internet telecast, I watched spellbound as military, government, and corporate witnesses told their stories in front of a packed audience at the National Press Club in Washington, D.C. All the major networks, plus the wire services, were present for the entire two-hour presentation. The witnesses talked about their experiences of tracking objects on radar, first-hand involvement with retrieving bodies from extraterrestrial craft, reverse engineering of ET craft, and the government's position on the whole subject.

I was absolutely amazed as I sat at my desk in Ridgway, Colorado, watching via the Internet. From studying the Urantia Book, I had learned of the trillions of sentient beings in the universe. Now I saw extraterrestrials not as something far off, but as here on my planet, in my backyard.

For the first time, I came to believe that extraterrestrials were real and were present on Earth. Neither television networks nor newspapers carried any reporting of this event.

The Disclosure Project had a profound effect on me. As I listened to the witnesses, I came to understand about a Larger Picture outside the conventional paradigm, a much larger picture. The reality of extraterrestrials interacting with humans in various ways moved me deeply, opened my eyes, and helped me understand that what I was writing about was more than science fiction. Moreover, I saw the conventional paradigm's refusal to admit to extraterrestrials was part of maintaining a tight rein on what people were allowed to believe, thus keeping them in cocoons that were prescribed by those in power.

During the last week of June in 2001, I joined a group of forty-seven people headed by Dr. Steven Greer (CSETI) in Crestone, Colorado. This group included my sister Gail. For the next week, we met as a group during the day, and then gathered in a circle in chairs under the night sky, so we could watch for paranormal phenomena in every direction. We were positioned in the San Luis

Valley, a high desert area south of Crestone, just west of the Sangre de Cristo mountain range, and north of the Sand Dunes National Park.

The first night out, I was seated, facing south, next to Steve. We had engaged the CSETI protocol, to ask ETs to join us, if it was convenient, in everyone's best interest, and beneficial. Suddenly I saw a laser light across my field of vision. Steve was pointing to an extremely bright star. "That's the starship of Kindness," a high-ranking extraterrestrial, Steve said to the group. I watched as the light corkscrewed upward, disappearing into the night sky. Others around the circle saw the same phenomenon.

A while later, it was now getting close to midnight, I looked to my left toward the mountains. There I saw four very distinct yellow squares, hanging in the night sky. They appeared as if they were lights of a passing train where someone had flicked on the lights. I watched, fascinated. Then I blinked and they were gone. "Did you see that?" I asked Steve. "Yes," he replied.

Now, when you are out at night, it is hard to tell distances, so I did not know if the yellow squares were smaller and close, or larger and far away. Nonetheless, I recall them quite distinctly, to this day. By that time, my excitement level was very high, and I was wide awake despite the late hour.

Later that same night, there were red and white lights on the lower side of Mount Blanca, south of our location. I watched as they appeared to come closer to our group. Almost all the others also saw them. By that time, I was shaking from head to toe. Then the lights backed off. "What happened?" I asked Steve. "They sensed that some in the group were not ready for them to make an appearance," he said. I got into bed that night about 3:00 AM.

The next day, we met as a group at the Lodge and watched a video of the Disclosure Project witnesses, and then had discussions about their testimony. I learned about the activities of the black ops, the ways in which certain activities of the government were being hidden, corporations that were involved in reverse engineering the technologies of crashed UFOs, and the ways in which the media systematically refused to report information about UFOs and ETs.

The next evening, after the group had settled into their chairs, at about dusk, a large hawk swung low, and circled just behind the chairs of the group. Later, a bright light in the southwest flashed back in response to Steve's laser. I saw a bright blue stick figure, about three feet in height, as it appeared next to the group. It was comprised of long top and bottom vertical pieces with a short cross member in the middle. I dismissed it until the next day, when others said they too had seen it.

The next night was clear with few clouds. The sky was filled with military search planes. The group meditated to construct a golden dome of protection over us. One of the cooks at the White Eagle Lodge saw the golden dome from a distance, and immediately quit his job.

The following night, two large, bright lights angled across the sky. They appeared to stop near the half moon in the west. Within minutes, two military jets screamed overhead, targeted toward that position in the sky. Not long after, the two ET craft blinked out.

The following morning, I was walking alongside the highway near the White Eagle Lodge. I had walked about 30 minutes. Suddenly a six-foot, clearly delineated, dark shadow appeared on the ground around me. The sun was to the east; the slightly elongated shadow appeared to be coming from the southwest. Later on the walk, a hawk descended to fly closely around my head. Steve interpreted these to be sure signs of contact.

On Thursday evening, we went to a new location, near Zapata Falls, a parking area on the side of Mount Blanca, overlooking the San Luis Valley to the north. After a while, it clouded up and began to rain. We all headed to our cars when the thunder and lightning began.

There were four in my car: myself, Gail, Gail's friend Anna, and another woman whose name I have lost. We were situated in a line of vehicles, overlooking the valley. About a hundred yards to my right was a sheer cliff side of Mount Blanca.

As we sat in our cars looking out through rain-streaked windows, my attention was called to the north. I yelled, "Look, look," and pointed out the right side windows.

I will never forget the brilliant blue lights of the craft as it emerged out of the side of the mountain. No, a portal did not open in the side of the mountain. The craft materialized, as it exited the solid rock. Then it flew out over the valley, and spurted into the atmosphere. Three of us in the car clearly saw the display, the fourth did not.

When the storm abated, the group got out of our cars. Only a few of the people in other vehicles had seen the craft. Steve said it was the sighting of a lifetime.

The final night that week, we saw an ET craft settle on the ground, a ways northeast from the group. It materialized itself enough to be visible in the moonlight. Later, it lifted off the ground, enough for us to see the lights of Crestone beneath it, lights it had previously hidden.

I had experienced so much the previous days that I glowed with new insights into the larger picture. It took several days for me to get my feet back on the ground. Heidi just smiled at my new way of seeing things, and the way I could not stop talking about them. She had encouraged me to undertake the CSETI experience by myself.

For the next three years, Heidi and I went back to Crestone. Once it was with only close associates of Steven Greer. One time, when we were seated in our circle and it was not yet dark, I felt someone bounce my chair. When I turned around, there was no one there. A few minutes later, others felt similar bouncing of their chairs. The ETs were telling us they were there, even if not visible.

One year I journeyed to a CSETI outing at Joshua Tree National Park, near Palm Springs, California. There I received a very clear message that I was to pay attention to my insights, my knowing, and my intuition. I recognized that I did this all the time, but wasn't paying attention. I made a decision to discern between sources that were real, and my imagination.

As Steve sat in the circle across from me, I saw two semi-physical beings on either side of him. I also saw a brilliant blue column of light in the center of the circle. At that moment, I received the following message, "You are being called to help transform this planet." This was one of the clearest communications I had received, to date.

Throughout all of my interactions with Dr. Steven Greer while looking for UFOs and becoming "Ambassadors to the Universe," I did not feel threatened or fearful. I did express my feelings to him that I was prepared to die to accomplish what I knew was my path. I credit him with spearheading publicity about the presence of extraterrestrials on our planet.

During the three years I interacted with him, he and I did not agree on the reality of divisive ETs, channeled information, or past lives. He attributed all dark ET activities to humans, and could not see how my books were anything other than my imagination. I now know that the vast majority of extraterrestrials in the universe are benevolent with higher consciousness, and that only a very small percentage, those in this sector of the Milky Way Galaxy, are self-centered, with a very diminished Light of Source.

For me personally, my involvement with Dr. Steven Greer and CSETI was a real turning point in my journey to higher consciousness. I now knew without a doubt that there were beings from other planets interacting with humanity in a variety of ways. I had seen their ships materialize and dematerialize, leading me to understand how vibration and frequency played with physical matter.

However, as much as I had modified my views of the conventional paradigm, at that time, I was still influenced by fear, anxiety, judgment, polarity, and drama. Love and unity were never discussed within the context of the Disclosure Project. My book, *Trillion*, despite what I had learned from others about humanity's current situation and my CSETI experience, was grounded in the fear, judgment and duality of the conventional paradigm.

During this period, Heidi and I lived in a spacious house in a beautiful location on a mesa facing the Sneffels Range, some of the most rugged mountains in Colorado. There was a large herd of elk that interrupted our journey to town, on more than one occasion. Another herd grazed very near the soccer field, on the other side of town.

We had deer in our yard every day, sometimes twice. The young ones wanted to play with Amber, our dog. Their mothers objected, with flying front hooves. We did not see any mountain lions, but the area was one of the few in Colorado where hunting of them was allowed. One neighbor told us he had seen one kill a deer, not far away.

Amber and I hiked every day. We lived at 8,000 feet of elevation in a heavily wooded area. Being a city boy, I had some trepidation about venturing out on my own. However, I soon became familiar with the roads and paths in our area. From time to time, I had the feeling we were being observed. I did find the large print of a mountain lion, in a snow patch near where we hiked.

My time with Amber was very special. We became very close. I now recall her often as I go about my daily life. Heidi and I have not found another dog, partially because Amber was so special.

Heidi and I fly fished in the many streams in Ouray County. We found one stream below Silver Jack reservoir, where we consistently caught as many trout as we wished to take home. We also fished on undisclosed local streams, usually catching enough, and always having fun. I always kept what I caught rather than throwing it back, injured and traumatized. I do not do "catch and release."

We skied frequently at Telluride, about forty-five minutes away. It is an old mining town with very expensive homes built on the side of the nearby hills. One of the most beautiful ski areas in Colorado, it was never crowded. I remember one Christmas Day when there were no lift lines at all.

During these years my web site became quite popular and I was contacted by over a hundred people who had experienced contact with ETs. Many of them had had these experiences since they were small children. Most of them found it both fearful and exciting, many of them welcomed it and wished it to continue. I spent many hours exchanging emails, on the telephone, dialoguing with people, and met a number in person. I found the listening ability that I had learned from my psychology degree was invaluable in connecting with them. I also found them grappling with the media and government's position about ETs, as they sought to resolve what they knew to be true. This dichotomy caused them both psychological and emotional problems, as they questioned their sanity, and made them reluctant to speak with others about it. They were most grateful to have someone with whom they could openly converse.

After Heidi finished teaching, we pulled a 5th wheel trailer around the United States, visiting twenty-nine states. First we took it to Roswell, where I made a presentation. Then it was off to Salt Lake City, where I spoke about ETs and the larger reality. Next we traveled to California, Oregon, Washington, Idaho, and finally, back to Colorado. I made presentations, and did workshops at each stop along the way.

We purchased a house in Fort Collins, Colorado, to have a base from which to operate. After a couple of months of winter, we headed to Florida to meet with friends, and I did another presentation. Then we worked our way up the East Coast, following spring, making presentations, until we arrived in New Jersey. There we connected with family. We went to New York City for my presentation to a wonderful group to whom I present annually.

The price of fuel edged higher and we decided to head to Colorado. After twenty-nine states, and almost as many get-togethers, book signings, workshops and presentations, we called a halt. Thinking it over, we sold our 5th wheel trailer, and I went back to writing my third book, *One.*

For the next three years, I focused on my writing. In addition, I conducted a workshop, thereby discovering a higher consciousness group, SPRE, as well as connecting to several people with whom I remain in contact. These all combined to expanding the setting for others to make presentations. Heidi and I spearheaded the effort, to rent the terminal of the abandoned airport near downtown Fort Collins. There we were quite successful at hosting a variety of speakers and showcasing videos. I watched as the energy of that old terminal building escalated with our higher consciousness events.

Gail, Anna, and I went back to the San Luis Valley by ourselves. We stayed at the Silver Star bed and breakfast in Crestone. Juelle and Donovan ran it. I did not know at the time that Juelle was a walk-in. Subsequently she has written a book, *The Walk-In*, that describes her experiences. I knew nothing about my situation, as a walk-in, at that time.

For the first two nights, Gail, Anna and I went to the area where CSETI groups had gathered. We were ready to engage extraterrestrial phenomenon. Using the CSETI protocol, we tried to call in craft. The energy both in the Baca and on the side of Mount Blanca was particularly still. We saw nothing and we sensed nothing.

The third night, thinking there was nothing to see, we decided to just sit on the balcony of the Silver Star and look out over the San Luis Valley for ET craft. After a couple of hours, I got tired and headed to my bedroom on the lower level.

The next morning at breakfast, Gail said to me, "You really missed it last night." I had no idea what she was talking about. It turned out that as soon as I had departed, they had wandered to the front of the Silver Star building. An ET craft had lighted up the entire landscape. Juelle and Donovan had also seen it.

I asked my higher self, "Why did I miss out on this?" The answer I got telepathically was, "You do not need to see any more phenomenon. You are already convinced of our reality. You are able to communicate directly with us." I did not know exactly what was meant by these words, but deep inside they seemed to satisfy me.

4

This chapter deals with a number of events and resources. It is designed to give you a better feel for who I am, in the Larger Picture. It is also designed to give you resources for your advancement to higher consciousness.

WEB SITE:

I established cosmicparadigm.com to sell books. Only within the last seven years have I learned just how appropriate is the name I used for it, "Cosmic Paradigm," to describe the vast reality that includes nonphysicals, how extraterrestrials are a part of this reality, and how all of this impacts humanity.

On my web site, I have presented several well known sightings of UFOs. They remain some of the best available: https://www.cosmicparadigm.com/ets-nonphysicals/

The messages I received from extraterrestrials, Celestial, and other important beings are also posted at www.cosmicparadigm.com. These will be available in Part III.

RADIO INTERVIEWS:

In the interests of marketing my books, I hired a publicity firm who provided me with a huge binder of information about how to position and market my book. This led me to a firm specializing in obtaining radio interviews. I was subsequently interviewed on

AM and FM radio over 150 times during the period 2003 to 2005, in virtually every major market and town of any size. This helped publicize my web site and sell books.

My first radio interview was with a small station, KVNF, in Paonia, Colorado, on May 23, 2002. The two hosts, Arlyn and Josh, and I had become friendly through mutual acquaintances. They started by talking about the Disclosure Project. Josh said that over 400 witnesses had come forth to testify and bring supporting evidence about the existence of UFOs, extraterrestrial vehicles, and advanced energy and propulsion technologies. He explained that the Disclosure Project was calling on Congress to hold hearings.

I talked about ETs visiting us to open us to the Larger Picture, and about my research to create my book. I said that *Trillion,* my first book, would soon be available. I played some sound clips from the Disclosure Project, and all three of us made comments.

After the hour was over, Josh was called into the station manager's office and fired, because the manager could not have "stuff like this" on his station.

I quickly found that radio hosts were uniformly interested in the sensational, and in my case that was UFOs, ETs, and the secret government. As long as I was talking about anything in this arena, I was regarded as an expert and invited back for further discussions. For a period of twenty-four months, I was very busy with interviews several times a week.

When I moved to suggesting that people take responsibility for what was going on, or that they look at how they were living, my ratings went down. People were interested in pending earth changes, how they should be prepared, and stories of contact with extraterrestrials. However, I discovered that few were doing anything as a result of what I was saying. I then realized that I was supplying entertainment, not delivering a message to be taken seriously.

NEWSLETTERS:

My newsletters of 2005 spoke to the transformation of Earth and humanity. I wrote that the people who were in control of the existing power structure would have us believe that it was business as usual, another day in the 3rd Dimension world, and things had always been this way. I saw the media and entertainment colossus spewing out pabulum to keep us happy according to the dictates of those in power.

Those who sensed the energies of change knew that we had the opportunity to create a higher functioning world, and that we were being coached and cheered onward by a massive gathering of extraterrestrial beings. I wrote about how I felt that my life had been orchestrated, events and people contributing to who I am.

Everyone's experience was valid, each interpretation of reality presenting a piece of a beautiful unfolding, like the instruments of an orchestra. I wrote that I was just beginning to appreciate how powerful my each and every thought was, and how extraordinarily powerful were our collective thoughts. I also expressed that there were no good or bad experiences, just experiences. If we could collectively focus our thoughts on creating a wonderful new world, we could create such. The hundredth monkey principle could then come alive.

I exhorted people to avoid the major media with its news about murders, terrorism, designer drugs, entertainment and gossip. Rather, they should hold their focus on a new planetary paradigm, the Cosmic Paradigm, and that we must prevail for the highest good of all in the Galaxy. And finally, I invited everyone to join the Cosmic Paradigm Network to add their voices to those dedicated to making this happen.

The next step was to take full responsibility for what happens. Send love and positive energy to the darkest of places. Walk your talk by living these steps.

By 2006 I was writing about political and economic conditions in the U.S. and global warming. I was saying that 97% of what people had grown up believing was not true, and that we were living in a fabricated reality. I recommended that they turn their backs on it as the single most important decision that they could make.

I wrote about Earth as a very special planet and how the drama playing out here reverberated throughout the universe. I wrote about Earth ascending to a higher dimension, and asked if people wanted to go with her or stay stuck in the 3rd Dimension.

I stated that it was very important for those who currently controlled the populations of this planet to continue to be acknowledged as the highest power on the planet. It was not in their best interests to admit that there are beings beyond this planet who know more, who might suggest different ways of behaving.

I proposed that if we really wanted to change this planet, then we must, first and foremost according to Gandhi, "become that which we wished the world to be." I found empowerment by merely suggesting these words, and thanked everyone for allowing me to express what was in my heart.

ALTERNATIVE PROGRAMS:

At the same time I was writing newsletters, conducting radio interviews, and making presentations, Heidi and I found several wonderful programs that contributed to our awareness of the larger picture, trained us to be part of an exciting new journey, and helped us to know who we really are.

Energetic Matrix was introduced in the book, *Sanctuary, The Path to Consciousness*, by Stephen Lewis and Evan Slawson. The program uses a Spiritual Technology to remove energy imbalances and follow a path to consciousness in order to attain and integrate emotional, physical and spiritual harmony. Heidi and I engaged in this program for a number of years and found it to be of great benefit in understanding and balancing our personal energies, and leading us to excellent health.

Remote Viewing is a mental faculty that allows a perceiver to describe or give details about a target that is inaccessible to normal senses due to distance, time, or shielding. Heidi and I received training in Remote Viewing, and once again it expanded our perception of reality.

Out-of-body Experiences explore human consciousness and expanded states of awareness. The Monroe Institute® (the leader in this discipline) enables individuals to experience targeted and expanded states of awareness. TMI program participants learn to access different states of awareness through this specially designed audio-guidance system. Both Heidi and I participated in out-of-body training to develop our abilities and found it a wonderful way to see things differently and to expand our consciousness. I have had success in achieving a state of nothingness, from which one can explore other levels of consciousness and can travel in time.

When I visited Charlottesville, Virginia, Heidi and I were hosted by Ed and Georgia. As we drove to their home we passed the Monroe Institute. I conducted a three-day workshop that was attended by about twenty highly conscious people. One of these was staying at Robert Monroe's house (Monroe had passed over). She offered to give me a private session.

As I walked in the door of Robert Monroe's house, I felt the energies of the many who had experienced out-of-body work there. When I laid out on Monroe's sofa, Red pulled in a group of non-humans who ran a scan over my body. It was very much like an MRI without the tunnel. I could feel the energies moving through my body. They said that my body was in fine shape, except for the big toe on my right foot. (Now I consistently wear out shoes where my right big toe rubs against the top of the inside.)

Matrix Energetics, the creation of Richard Bartlett, is about transforming beliefs concerning healing, disease, and the structure of reality. It is based on the expression of subtle energy physics and the concepts and laws of quantum physics and superstring theory. Participants often see and feel a wave-like motion when Matrix Energetics is applied, as the person being worked on experiences a smooth wave of transformation and the body seems to drop into a completely relaxed wave instantly. Participants are taught specific methods of using powerful, focused intent. Heidi and I received training in this discipline, and practice it whenever we feel our bodies out of alignment.

We went to a one-week training session in Denver. The first morning, Dr. Bartlett asked for a volunteer who was an engineer to come onto the stage. Heidi pointed me out. With some reservations, I climbed onto the stage and faced Dr. Bartlett.

He welcomed me and, shaking his head, said, "Where are you? Oh, there you are." He reached high above me in a gesture to retrieve my energy. Then, with no preparation, he demonstrated the power of Matrix Energetics by facing the palms of his hands towards me. He did not touch me. Momentarily unconscious, I collapsed onto the stage and into the arms of his assistant. I lay on the stage, dazed as he went on with his lecture.

By the end of that first day, the energy of the conference room became such that I was able to approach people and lay them onto its carpeted floor. The rest of the week, we learned techniques to remove unwanted energies for both our own and the bodies of others, thus healing many physical problems.

For several months thereafter, a group of Matrix Energetics students gathered at our home to practice/play with what we had learned. There have been many reported healings as a result of applying Matrix Energetics tools. I am a case in point. I highly recommend this course.

PRESENTATIONS:

In 2002, I made my first stand-up presentation. My friend, Robin, the director of the Telluride, Colorado library, had set me up in a small room. I held a copy of my first book, *Trillion*, and had copies of it for sale at the back of the room.

It was an audience of mostly friends. Even though I was an accomplished public speaker, in other venues, the material in the book was so extreme, and I was so shy about it, that I was unable to speak the words ET or extraterrestrial. Instead, I stuck to the story line and the setting in Arizona.

A few months later, in my January 2003 presentation, I talked about the transformation of the planet, in terms of stopping violence and creating a sustainable environment. I presented significant ET events, such as the Battle of Los Angeles, the Roswell Crash, Billy Meier, the Rendlesham Incident, Belgium Triangles, the Phoenix Lights, the Disclosure Project, and the Turkish Meteor Incident. (All available at *www.cosmicparadigm.com*)

I emphasized that we were not the only inhabited planet, that we were misreading ET contact as fearful. I said that visitors from other planets were here to assist the most important event in our history, our transformation.

I finished up by saying that extraterrestrial contact is about truth, and whether or not we will let its truth motivate us. I emphasized that extraterrestrials were nothing like what Hollywood would have us believe. This leads people to attribute to extraterrestrials, jokingly or seriously, what they do not understand.

In my March 2004 presentation, at the Aztec UFO Conference, I added the cover-up of extraterrestrial contact, and the broader implication of it. I pointed out that it was our xenophobia that automatically caused us to regard ETs as something to be feared. I insisted that many top government officials know what is going on.

There is a concerted effort to cover up the truth about ETs, as those in power know that the truth will likely change the world power structure.

My presentation pointed out that we are more than our physical body. We possess uniqueness, memory, soul, a superconscious, and intuition. We are capable of out-of-body travel, remote viewing, and telepathy.

I talked about being trapped in a psychological box created by my ego. It manifested itself as busy, focused, preoccupied, fearful, self-centered, and rational. (I now refer to this as a cocoon.)

I asked the members of the audience to dismiss their boxes. Share with others what they knew about the larger truth. And finally, that in order to be accepted by the other worlds of the cosmos, the people of this planet must awaken to a new level of consciousness.

In my presentations a year later, I had added that the experience of contact with ETs took many forms, and that it could be spiritual. I pointed out that extraterrestrial contact was going on all over the world, and that there was a concerted effort to cover it up through ridicule and fear. I showed a recent survey, in which 12% of those surveyed said that they had experienced contact with UFOs, and in which 72% believed the government was not telling the truth.

I introduced the idea that ETs were on a spectrum that included spiritual beings. I talked about out-of-body experiences, and remote viewing, as ways to touch our non-physical selves and universe consciousness.

I spent some time talking about our troubled planet: melting Arctic icecaps, destruction of tropical rainforest, pollution of air, water and land, violence, injustice, and a worldwide conspiracy to maintain the status quo.

By the time of my presentations later that year, I had added that this moment was the pivotal juncture in human history. I stated that each person experiences contact with non-human life forms through his or her own filter. I again said that contact with extraterrestrials can be profoundly spiritual.

I presented pictures, showing paintings from the Middle Ages that depicted flying craft, and pointed out that there were no hot air balloons or airplanes at that time. I talked about other countries being more open, about sightings of ET craft, and that less than 1% of contactees reported "abduction" experiences.

I talked about how Colonel Philip J. Corso gave technology from downed ET craft to private corporations, and how it was reverse engineered to give us things like semiconductors and light fiber cables.

During the years 2003 to 2007, I made presentations to groups in Los Angeles and Redwood City, California; Salt Lake City, Salem, Oregon; Roswell, New Mexico; Laughlin, Nevada; Vancouver, B.C.; Fort Collins and Denver, Colorado; Orlando and Miami, Florida; Chicago, New York, Charlottesville, Virginia; Montreal, Quebec, and San Jose, Costa Rica.

One of my most memorable experiences took place in San Jose, the capital of Costa Rica. Two wonderful women, Karen and Bonnie, had read *Trillion*, and invited me to present a three-day workshop.

When I arrived, I was interviewed by a reporter, and then taken to the offices of the largest newspaper in San Jose. As it turned out, the editor wanted to meet me, so he could tell me of his experiences. That evening, I was on national television, talking about extraterrestrials. I was a front page story in the newspaper the next day. What a difference from the way in which the media here in the U.S. treats the subject.

The venue for my workshop was a former brewery, with 6-foot thick stone walls, in downtown San Jose. The room accommodated about thirty. At that time, I was talking about the reality of extraterrestrials, and that they were here to assist in our transformation. I also went through a series of exercises to help people understand who they were in relationship to the larger paradigm. Looking back on that workshop, I now see that I was just beginning to understand what extraterrestrials and ET craft were all about, and the broader implications of their activities among us.

The Dalai Lama had been in San Jose the prior week, meeting with his Lamas from around the world. A Lama from Barcelona, Spain, attended my second day. At the lunch break, he asked if he could speak to the group. After we were all reassembled, he said, "What Mr. Kimmel is saying to you is exactly what we understand." He told me privately that they seldom talked about this subject.

I have been back to Costa Rica several times, with Heidi, to meet with the wonderful, highly conscious people there. Karen, the closest to an earth-bound angel I've ever met, and her husband Sam, author and very insightful, are always the perfect hosts during our stay. Each time, I present my latest to a group organized by them.

Once I was invited to address the graduate students at LaSalle University in San Jose. They were pursuing Ph.D. degrees in the New Paradigm. (Is this great or what?). As I was entering the auditorium for that presentation, I was introduced to Rolando Araya, a prominent national politician. He said that he was disappointed that he could not be present for my talk, but that he was scheduled at a meeting in the adjoining auditorium.

A group of us journeyed to Arenal, an active volcano, a couple of hours north of San Jose. I watched as huge chunks of red lava crashed down the side of the mountain, splintering trees in the forest below.

We looked at a piece of land near Arenal, upon which to establish an institute for peace and the new paradigm. On the way back to San Jose, I was seated up front with the driver of the van. It began raining and he could not get the opening in the roof closed.

So every time we took a curve or stopped, I shouted, "aqua fria," as water from the roof drenched me. Upon returning to the U.S., I received a strong message to remain in the U.S., rather than moving to Costa Rica.

I began my 2005 presentation at the Roswell Anniversary Celebration, with the words, "Ninety-nine percent of what you grew up believing is a lie." Then I talked about the metamorphic transformation of the planet, and that we were pawns in a multi-dimensional chess game.

I talked about crop circles being communications from extra-terrestrials, and showed a short video of an orb forming one in a matter of minutes.

I told how Margaret Thatcher had cautioned author, Georgina Bruni, on revealing the truth about ETs, saying, "You can't tell the people." These words became the title of her book.

I showed an Egyptian relief of 1,500 B.C. that depicted flying craft. I talked about the ancient tablets from Sumeria that exposed ET contact, including enslavement and bioengineering.

I proposed that some UFO sightings were holographic projections, and that 80% of physical sightings were of man-made craft.

I defined the current paradigm as most people being asleep to the larger reality. I suggested that everyone had volunteered to come into his or her body, at this time and place, and that it was one of many incarnations. I said that we were players, on an Earthly stage erected for our experiences.

I showed pictures of a deteriorating planet. I recommended survival supplies of food and water, storing gold, and maintaining a healthy body. I pointed out that we see the world through our beliefs, and how these beliefs color everything we see, think, and do, and how our collective beliefs are leading to planetary destruction.

My list of nine recommendations for those present were to see the world for what it was, turn away from the existing paradigm, recognize the larger reality, accept that we are each extraordinarily powerful, envision a better world, hold that vision, affirm a better world by living it, know that non-human life forms are assisting us, and join with others of like mindset.

I announced the Cosmic Paradigm Network, for people who wanted to contribute to the transformation.

I spoke before an audience of about 600 at the March 2006 International UFO Congress, presenting myself as a "suit," who had made a one-eighty to where I was today, and that I had dedicated myself to this path full time since 1996.

In addition to things I had in my earlier presentations, I showed a chart that depicted the existing paradigm. It molded who we were and what we believed, as a combination of: government, religion, media, financial institutions, history, science, medicine, and education.

I talked about my experiences with CSETI. I talked about how my first book, *Trillion*, after extensive editing and ready for publishing, had required almost no changes after my UFO sightings with the CSETI group in June of 2001. This indicated to me that I had received considerable help in writing it. I said that people who had read it considered it to be insightful and prophetic.

I stated that the Hopi, whose culture is dated back to 4000 BCE on Mesa 1, had made Kachina dolls to represent the gods (ETs?) who inhabited San Francisco Peak, north of Flagstaff, Arizona, and who had taught them to farm corn, beans, and squash.

I referenced an Aurora, Texas newspaper from 1897. Its front page was filled with articles about flying ships, and the beings who had come from them.

I showed several pictures of crop circles, and talked about the strange electromagnetic readings that were obtained inside them.

I talked about the over 200 people who had contacted me by telephone, email and letters, with their stories of contact and wanting more; people who had experiences from a very young age; people who recalled lives prior to the one in this body; and walk-ins. I said that the vast majority of the people I communicated with had benign experiences.

I stated that I believed that ETs were highly evolved, had seeded life here. Some had been involved in our enslavement, and that some were here to "assist" us, but not save us. I foresaw a spiritual awakening, and that we were in our final days, before huge changes would occur.

I talked about the many secret psychological and biological experiments that had been carried out by our government on unsuspecting and/or unwilling humans. I listed all the executive orders that curtail our individual freedoms.

I likened our current plight to those of indentured servants. Living from paycheck to paycheck. Fifty percent of earnings to taxes. Little or no savings. Stresses. Believing that this is as good as it gets. Numbed by TV, movies, books, and news. Personal freedoms curtailed. Sending children off to war. Believing in rewards in heaven. That an elite group was in control.

I said that we were non-physical life forms who incarnated in physical bodies, and that my physical body was a projection from the non-physical. I laid out the components of my non-physical body as astral, fragment of divinity, higher self, soul, spirit, and superconscious. I said that I chose to incarnate, to play this role, that all were choosing their experiences. I said that my divinity fragment chose this body to experience life in a new way, to evolve my soul. I said that we were extraordinarily powerful, and that a dedicated few can evolve the human presence on this planet.

I proposed a new paradigm consisting of a larger reality, unlimited free energy, unlimited wealth, sustainable environment, personal responsibility, telepathic communications, health, Creator's plan, and cosmic citizens. I asked for the members of the audience to follow this plan: sustainable, wake up, responsible, embrace power, hold vision, loving observer, living example. I invited everyone to join the Cosmic Paradigm Network.

I received a standing ovation.

In the months that followed, my frequency of presentations slowed dramatically as I focused on finishing the third book,

One, of the *Paradigm Trilogy.* In a 2007 presentation, my focus had changed dramatically in the course of one year. UFOs and ETs are barely mentioned. I used words from others, to give my presentation authenticity. I see a higher level of my own fear coming out in these presentations, compared to just a year earlier. I suggested that Earth shifts and extreme weather would result in chaos, affecting people's lives, and they should prepare for it by storing food and water, holding gold, living sustainably, and seeking out a "safe" place to live. I focused on the wealthy and powerful elites who operate a secret government. I laid out the various ways in which we the people were controlled.

Based on input from others and my own experiences in the business world, I attributed phrases like the following to the "elites:" "It's mine, and I'll do whatever I want with it." "The world is hostile. Those people gotta be controlled." "It all comes down to economics." "This is just the way things are."

I referenced the book, *The Creature From Jekyll Island,* and its thesis about money and the Federal Reserve. I quoted President Woodrow Wilson as stating, "Some of the biggest men in the United States, in the field of commerce and manufacture, are afraid of something. They know there is a power so organized, so subtle, so watchful, so interlocked, so complete, so pervasive, that they had better not speak above their breath when they speak in condemnation of it."

I quoted David Rockefeller as saying, "We are on the verge of a global transformation. All we need is the right major crisis, and the nation will accept the New World Order."

I pointed out that the elites, through their wealth and power, and through influence over people in key positions, controlled: the media, economy, religions, psychology, education, medicine, history, government, and corporations.

I introduced the idea that Earth had begun as God's special paradise, that we had ET ancestors, that there were dark souls and light souls, and that the truth about all was slowly coming out. I presented the Hopi Elders' prophecies about imminent earth changes as being very accurate. I predicted extreme weather and higher ocean levels due to melting ice.

I talked about the work of Dr. Masaru Emoto in freezing water to show the influence of thought, positive or negative, upon it. I stated that everything is energy and that my thoughts can control it. I talked about our oversouls and how they were the accumulator of experiences from our various lifetimes and the orchestrator thereof. I stated that my soul is unique and my free will is preeminent.

I quoted Abraham Hicks: "The Universe is not punishing you or blessing you. The Universe is responding to the vibrational attitude that you are emitting."

Finally, I suggested that they should: Reject The Elitist Paradigm—Be Sustainable—Embrace The Power Of Who You Really Are—Hold The Vision of a New Civilization—Join with ETs and Celestials—Create Community.

After receiving a strong warning about dangers from earth changes and the collapse of the conventional paradigm—all given by people of high conscious—Heidi and I began to look for a new place to live away from Fort Collins. She and I each took a trip to southwest Colorado, looking for a house and a community. My brother, Brian, had lived in the area for a number of years and sang its praises.

On the way home from a visit with Brian, I began to get messages. I well remember driving along mountain roads on my way back to Denver, while I scribbled in my notebook about how Pagosa Springs would be a good place to settle, because of the spiritual community that existed there.

On one trip to Pagosa, Heidi and I were invited to a get-together with thirty other people, all of whom were well aware of extraterrestrials. When we returned to Fort Collins, Steve, the host of the get-together, tracked me down and said, "The beings you communicate with are the same ones I talk to. I'm supposed to get to know you." This sealed it for us. We went home and put our Fort Collins home on the market.

At one point, those who were communicating with me told me to set up a new web page, "Athabantian," so that I could post their messages free of my rational mind's commentary. The quality of my automatic writing took a step upward. I set up a second page, "Perspectives," where I could post my opinions without interfering with the many messages from extraterrestrials, Celestials, and others that I posted at Athabantian.

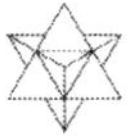

BOOKS:

The Paradigm Trilogy began with *Trillion.* As I said earlier, the beginnings of this book spilled out of my computer in 1997 as I was writing an academic paper for my psychology degree. It was written in story form because I was familiar with that style of writing, although I had never written anything like a story before. I wove what I knew about the larger picture into the story line.

I established "Paradigm Books," set up "Cosmic Paradigm" as my web site, and went off with Dr. Steven Greer to my first CSETI week.

After my week in the San Luis Valley, I had only one change to make in a book about extraterrestrials, a book that had been created before I saw my first UFO. Einstein had said nothing can travel faster than the speed of light. I found out how the ETs do it: They dematerialize. I had seen them do it. I now knew it was simply a matter of controlling vibration level.

I found a local woman to format my book. I ordered 2,000 hard-back copies of *Trillion.* I still remember the day the truck showed up in downtown Ridgway, Colorado with the heavy boxes. The truck could not get to the top of the mesa on the dirt roads where we lived, so I loaded the heavy boxes into the rear of my Jeep Cherokee and made several trips to my garage. Heidi and I spent the following months wrapping and mailing books to purchasers all over the U.S. and in other countries.

Trillion is about a group of extraterrestrials who live in the desert of Arizona. Their mission is to help humanity evolve so that Earth can become a full member of the benevolent universe. The protagonist is an entrepreneur from Boulder, Colorado who, initially, has no concept of extraterrestrials or civilizations beyond Earth.

Decimal, my second book, was published in 2004 because I had much too much information for my first book. By then, *Trillion* was in paperback and selling on Amazon, through other distribution channels, and from my web site. My radio interviews, but most particularly, my stand-up presentations were key to selling both books.

Decimal, also in story form, delves into the elites who control governments and corporations. It explores reverse-engineering of ET craft by secret government agencies and corporations, and the broader implications of that technology.

One was published in 2008. It tells the story of massive earth changes, total disruption of the government, and a false-flag invasion by spacecraft produced by humans. (Looking back from my current level of consciousness, I can see fear behind messages in the book.)

INSTITUTE OF LIGHT:

When Heidi and I moved to Pagosa Springs, Colorado, we found over a hundred conscious individuals who had "parties," where they congregated to discuss what was happening in the bigger picture and alternate news. We found that the messages I was posting, and the presentations I was making, correlated well with their level of consciousness, and we were welcomed into the group.

Soon after moving to Pagosa in 2009, I created a men's group. I had had some success with such a group when I lived in Boulder, and wished to see what I could get started here. There were conscious men in the town, but they were not focused.

This congenial group of men, including Dan, John, Russ, Hassyo, Peter, Albert, and Tom, met weekly for a period of five years, initially at coffee shops. We discussed everything from national politics to local happenings, from earth changes, to extraterrestrials, to spirituality. Sometimes the discussion was fear-based and judgmental. Most times we maintained a higher consciousness. Very seldom was there consensus, but we kept gathering each week.

In 2011 it was suggested by my Celestial contacts that I open a formal office for my work, so that I might meet people coming to me for counseling and connecting to extraterrestrials. I undertook the necessary course of study, and received my degree in Divinity from Universal Brotherhood Movement, to help get a not-for-profit entity. With that in hand, I created a Colorado corporation by the name of "The Institute of Light," and applied for a 501(c)3 designation from the IRS.

The men's group saw this as an opportunity to have a quiet space in which to meet each week. They offered to chip in their weekly coffee money, to help me pay for the rental of a larger space for IOL. This enabled me to rent something large enough to show movies, and to showcase visiting personalities.

The idea for a conference also sprang from messages I was receiving from Celestials, Adrial and Taugth, and our conversations around the table at IOL. In early 2012, we picked a date in August, began to round up speakers, and started to promote the event. It was not an easy task as the city of Pagosa Spring's population was only 1,200.

About that time I was given a vision of myself in a full-length white robe with a gold belt, not unlike the robe of a monk. I was traveling throughout the universe without a spaceship. I have not, as yet, purchased a robe. I am quite sure it was indicative of my role, as a wayshower embracing the material in Part IV of this book.

I found local people willing to donate their time and expertise. Tom, one of the men in the men's group, fronted the event with a

$4,000 loan. I hired a very experienced sound technician, who just happened to be local. A local hotel with a large conference room, a restaurant, and plenty of guest rooms, gave us a special rate for the three days.

"The Transformation 2012" Conference attracted 150 people, eighty percent traveling from afar, including three foreign countries. At its conclusion, many reported that it was the best conference they had ever attended.

We had 15 speakers over the course of three days including: G. W. Hardin, Dr. Norma J. Milanovich, Suzy Ward, Itasha, Sonya Lugo, Celestial Blue Star and David of Arcturus, Don Daniels, Ron Radhoff, Uqualla, and Janet Purcell.

As I wrote these words, I received the following message:

The Institute (of Light) was an anchor involving a collective of people joining their intentions and actions together to ground the energies of change. It was a focal point in our efforts to assist humanity.

As I see it now, the Institute of Light was the culmination of a journey that had begun with my awakening and the word, "institute," coupled with my later discovery of extraterrestrials and the larger picture. But the journey was far from over, because I was still basing my thoughts and actions in fear, drama, polarity, and judgment while at the same time talking about a higher way to live. In other words, I had no clear basis from which I could inform others about the path to higher dimensions, because I was not following that path myself.

CONVENTIONAL PARADIGM:

I believe it is important to recognize the environment and background in which we, the humans of Earth, live. I say this, not from the viewpoint of inducing fear. Rather, knowing the truth gives you and me a foundation for knowing and acting, rather than merely believing what the media, books, or videos may be saying to you, or what someone else may have told you.

Many aspects of our lives are controlled by those who do not want the highest good of all; they do not recognize all members of humanity, let alone those in the universe, as their brothers and sisters, and they do not function from a place of complete Unity. Source's Love is rarely mentioned by those in the conventional paradigm. I now present a few paragraphs dealing with the darker aspects of the current paradigm.

Many people have interacted with me because of my web site, my radio interviews, my books, and my presentations. Because of this, I have accumulated information on the programs and activities that are dedicated to preserving the status quo. These programs are designed to benefit those in positions of power and wealth, versus everyone else. Some of them involve cooperation with detrimental extraterrestrials. I only summarize them here, because they are extensive enough to fill several books, and because I do not want to give undo energy to them.

We have many government entities that do not work on behalf of the populace, despite what they publicly report, or because they are secret. Fred Burks (*PEERS*) uncovers and publishes such activities. According to Catherine Austin Fitts (*The Solari Report*), there is $21 TRILLION that cannot be accounted for. Dr. Steven Greer (CSETI) regularly speaks about secret government programs.

Jim Marrs, author of the book *Rule by Secrecy*, says, "The real movers and shakers of the world collude to start and stop wars, manipulate stock markets and interest rates, maintain class distinctions, and censor the six o'clock news. They do this under the auspices of the Council on Foreign Relations, the Trilaterial Commission, the Bilderbergers, the CIA, and even the Vatican."

Terry Hansen, author of *The Missing Times*, pointed out ways in which information about ETs was being hidden by the media:

censorship, threats, harassment, high-level contacts, recruiting journalists, confiscation of evidence, character assassination, and incarceration.

Brave people like these provide insights into the agenda of the few who seek to maintain the status quo. Others focus on reptilians, as they infiltrate and influence individuals in government, corporations and all other institutions. While exposing these programs and activities, we have little ability to act against them using conventional methods; this is due to secrecy, deceit, distractions, and violence, plus our virtual captivity by manipulations and misinformation designed to escalate fear. For me, status quo refers to maintaining these structures, organizations, and laws of the current paradigm. This situation that does not involve Love or Unity, nor are they even mentioned.

In the United States we live in a very dysfunctional society, and other countries are not far behind in structuring everything for the benefit of the few versus the many. Those in positions of power adhere to few moral restraints, as witnessed by the exposure of pedophiles, women who have been molested, and manipulations to influence legal judgments. The United States has the highest prison population in the world. Politicians regularly dismiss mass shootings as the actions of a deranged person, and adhere to their mantra about the value of guns. The top three Americans have more wealth than the bottom 50%. Those acting behind the scenes use mind control, blackmail, money, and physical threats, to control people elected to positions of power and influence. We have the best Congress that money can buy, due to campaign laws that favor money over individuals.

Whistleblowers are persecuted for disclosing things that the public needs to know. Those who have insights into secret projects, publicize the truth about things like: weather control, the Illuminati, false flags like 9/11, the environmental crisis, illegal drug trade, drug resistant bugs, BRICS, and continuing problems with Fukushima.

Wealthy and powerful people enjoy the benefits of living in

the current paradigm, while they quietly influence the workings of governments in their favor. The uber-wealthy of the financial world wish for the status quo, as do those who are in control of major corporations. Although there are many dedicated medical professionals, the current medical system is designed to enrich physicians and drug companies first, care for patients second.

Those who buy into the programs promulgated by the elites, even though these programs impact themselves negatively, buoy up control of the rest of humanity by the elites. Major banks, in conjunction with federal agencies, are manipulating the monetary system, the stock market, and the price of gold.

Many of the stories about dark extraterrestrials, black ops, torture, mind control, psychotronics, human-manufactured star craft, secret underground bases, hybrid humans, clones, satanic cults, implants, pedophiles, and the controlled media, are true. Others are exaggerations and misinformation, disguised to confuse the truth, while exalting the power of those engaged in those activities.

Some of those who pursue this agenda do so in conjunction with detrimental extraterrestrials. Others are simply following a lifestyle that results from power and wealth. It is all based on the 3rd Dimension, on its continuation or evolution. Again, there is no mention of Love or Unity.

I know elites, and wannabe elites, who are straining to maintain their positions of wealth and power. They are fearful of what lies ahead. I also know many who aspire to that elevated status, and many more who are convinced that their lives will benefit from the agendas of the elites. There is never an admission by them, that we are all brothers and sisters.

Depictions of extraterrestrials in science fiction movies and on television show them as 3rd Dimension physical beings. In reality detrimental extraterrestrials are just that, they still possess physical bodies. They have not evolved to higher states of consciousness. They feed off the energy of fear that is produced by the human population of Earth. Some of the depictions are true; others are exaggerations. Their drama always depicts entities in conflict with one another. Unconditional Love and perfect Unity are never shown in science fiction presentations, or in science fiction writing. Higher consciousness is not a consideration. The published intent of these presentations is to entertain; the reality is that they produce fear in the individuals who view the conflict and violence.

Keep in mind that dark beings have had hundreds of thousands, if not millions, of years to develop advanced technologies. At the same time they are limited by their low levels of consciousness. They function based on fear, and would have all else function on that same basis. They have not evolved spiritually.

A major thrust of the dark entities, who are involved with human institutions such as government and media, is to control human perception. They have been successful in this by limiting the possibilities that people believe are open to them, thus making the "same old, same old," seem like the only path.

I am being told that I should not paint dark ETs with too broad a brush, because they are only operating from their level of consciousness. Understanding that we are all brothers and sisters of Source, we can send them Love.

The following conversation was with Archangel Michael. It offers a glimpse of a higher way to see things of the Conventional Paradigm and Larger Picture.

Good Afternoon, Michael.

Good afternoon, Mark.

I wish to inquire about the extraterrestrials, those who are called dark, those with very little Light of Source.

Yes, Mark, I will be happy to comment on those beings. It is okay to label them as dark, because they do indeed have little of the Light of Source within them.

Do they have the ability to be other than rigid physical form?

Yes, they have technology that allows them to shield their physical form. This, however, is different from operating at a higher consciousness. Their technology influences the mind of those with whom they interact, to make them appear to be without physical form, or in a different physical form.

So it is not a fundamental change in their make-up, rather it is how they appear to others?

That is correct.

It must be very powerful technology, to make them invisible to human eyes and human instruments.

It is indeed powerful.

How does this compare to functioning at higher energy?

When one is functioning at higher energy, higher consciousness, it is easy for their senses and mind to see them as non-physical. Thus, you can go to 5th Dimension, but your body is not yet able to hold you in 5th Dimension.

Are the dark ETs able to create human clones?

Yes. They can create human forms, but they are without souls that have been expressed from an oversoul.

Can dark ETs then inhabit these physical forms?

Yes.

Is there a way to detect a clone?

Only by seeing if they are functioning from fear versus Love.

How is this different from human who is in a state of fear?

It is not too different, in that a human who is functioning from a state of fear has very little of Source's Light within. So they are at the same energy level as dark ETs. Thus they can easily relate to each other at this fear-based physical level.

Am I missing something here?

The difference between a dark ET and a dark human (both of whom have little of Source's Light) is that an ET has access to technologies that enable him or her to travel interstellar, and enable the cloning and shielding of form. It is this ability that dark humans wish to acquire.

Do dark ETs have a soul?

Yes, but it is far removed from their bodies, because there is such a difference in energy levels. Contrast this with your soul that integrated into your body.

Are the images, that some see of dark ETs, what they really look like?

Those that see from a place of fear will conjure up appearances that match the fear they are expressing, thus the images will be of fearful beings. Contrast this with the form that you might attach to a higher consciousness ET. Because you are broadcasting Love, that form will appear to be quite friendly and beautiful.

Even when I look at dark ETs?

Mark, you will not encounter dark ETs because of your high-energy consciousness.

Thus, a demonstration of the power of energies?

Yes.

Thank you, Michael. I know you are with me as I write.

That is so. Blessings, Mark.

Blessings, Michael.

IN SUMMARY: I see in my radio shows and newsletters an eagerness to provide what I had discovered about extraterrestrials and the Larger Picture, to all who would listen. This set me on a path of disclosing information, rather than selling books. I have pursued this focus, full time, since then, selling just enough books to roughly break even. This has been reinforced by my non-physical friends, who tell me that they really don't care how many books I sell; what is important to them is my grounding of the information in words of the books. The revelations and my experiences with nonphysicals, that I will reveal in Part IV, have only intensified my commitment to this path.

My years involved with seeing UFOs, and feeling the presence of extraterrestrials, as I wrote and received messages, moved me from the depths of the conventional paradigm. It contributed to understanding the reality of a universe filled with sentient life forms, and exposed me to an Earthly world of lies, misrepresentations, secrets, and violence.

I now know that beneficial extraterrestrials make their presence known in the form of holographic UFOs to awaken us. Detrimental extraterrestrials try to seed fear in humanity by the presence of their craft, and stories of abductions, while working with some humans to undermine and control our civilization. Within secret projects, humans have successfully reverse-engineered ET craft. There is a secret government and there are black ops; neither work for the greater good of all.

One of the major benefits from my years of observing UFOs, and my time with CSETI, was an understanding of the role that higher energies played. I have seen ET craft materialize, dematerialize, and present themselves as partially physical. This was a big step to my later interactions with non-physical beings, and understanding the vast non-physical cosmos, and non-form.

Looking back from my current perspective, I see that in my earlier presentations I introduced concepts that are valid from my current perspective. However, today I would present them differently, based on my higher consciousness:

- Transformation of our planet
- Non-physical life forms incarnated in physical bodies
- Reverse-engineering of ET craft
- Crop circles
- A spiritual awakening
- Beneficial extraterrestrials assisting humanity
- Being trapped in a cocoon created by others
- A spectrum of extraterrestrials and spiritual beings
- Extraterrestrials' historical involvement with Earth
- Dark extraterrestrials

I also see several points that I made that are not in line with my current understanding:

- A multi-dimensional chess game. From my current understanding, this is not true, for highly consciousness extraterrestrials function based on Love and Unity. They do not engage in competition.
- An overwhelming dark energy. My current understanding is that there is no such dark energy, rather dark extraterrestrials are lower consciousness beings who are operating on the basis of fear and their own self-interest.
- We were in our final days before huge changes would occur and I recommended survival supplies of food and water, and storing gold. I now know that the change has been ongoing, since the time of these presentations, and it will continue to be gradual rather than happening in an instant. I see my survival recommendations coming from my own place of fear. While I see a time of chaos ahead, I would recommend a plan based on preparedness, not fear.
- Earth shifts, extreme weather, and higher ocean levels creating chaos. I do not foresee any of these affecting large portions of humanity, for we have raised consciousness enough that Earth no longer requires them as part of her ascension.

- A new Earth, based on extrapolating from what is current, plus adding unlimited free energy, unlimited wealth and sustainability. I now see a completely transformed Earth as humanity ascends to higher levels of consciousness. This is opposed to extrapolating from our current paradigm.

I see my presentations evolving. I believe I was functioning at a 4th Dimension level in that fear, judgment, polarity and guilt were present but not driving my words. I see many of my insights were amazingly good. I found that I really enjoyed, and still do, developing concepts for a presentation and standing in front of an audience and telling them what I believe to be true.

The three books of the *Paradigm Trilogy, Trillion, Decimal* and *One*, were written in story form. For these books I created characters to portray the extraterrestrials who walk this planet, seeking to assist humanity. I wove into these three adventure stories my understanding of the larger universe where extraterrestrials reside, my belief that there are people within the world's governments who are in collusion with certain extraterrestrials who seek to control humanity, my belief that humans have reverse engineered ET craft, and that such human spacecraft have nothing to do with NASA's programs.

Nowhere in the books of the *Trilogy* was there any mention of either Lemuria or Atlantis. I now know the importance of these two ancient civilizations. (As we shall see later.)

Nonetheless, looking back, I am amazed at how insightful I was in that period about the bigger picture, about secret operations in government and corporations, and about environmental destruction. I have since refined my message, as you will see in later chapters, but my urging people to become involved with Earth's transformation is still my message.

Please keep in mind that the three books of the *Paradigm Trilogy*, my newsletters, and the presentations I made prior to 2008, all took place before my communications with extraterrestrials began. I may have been getting assistance, but I was only vaguely aware of it.

And finally, I am convinced, now more than ever, that the only way out of the Conventional Paradigm, and the Larger Picture, is by raising the consciousness of humanity, so that we operate from a different platform. Anything less is a recipe for repeating the same old, same old, or maybe something worse.

PART III

Communications

5

What follows is a treasure trove, of insights and observations, from our star brothers and sisters, Celestials, and Yeshua. It encompasses humanity, Earth, our place in the universe and much more. I learned so much from these messages. There is no doubt that they raised my level of consciousness.

I believe it is critical that everyone understand what is really going on within our civilization, our countries, and our communities. I do this, not to encourage fear, rather to inform you. The following observations, from those who view humanity from outside our lives, will peel back the trappings of the conventional paradigm to expose the working of those who seek to control humanity for their own agenda. At the same time, these messages offer uplifting ways to act beyond the conventional paradigm.

Channeling: When I first started receiving communications, I was pretty unconscious. I was, after all, recently retired from my career in the world of business. Plus, my rational mind was going full tilt, trying to convince me that all of this extraterrestrial stuff was my imagination, and not to post things for which people would call me crazy.

A somewhat limited perspective can be seen in my older channeling and automatic writing, based on my interactions with physical phenomenon. In contrast, I see that the work I have done these last few years with the nonphysicals has opened me to a broader perspective; I am now able to receive messages from extraterrestrials much more clearly than before, and can now receive communications directly from non-physical beings.

I can see the influences of backgrounds and beliefs in the channelings of others, be it their religion, problems in their lives, their socio-economic situation, their careers, their insights into secrets, or their fears. No one is completely free of these influences; it comes with being in physical form.

I also see some who comment on the channeling of other people. Some come from a higher dimension and approach the difficulties attendant with channeling from the viewpoint of love. Others come from a lower consciousness, so they view channeled information based on their particular influences, or deny the validity of channeling altogether. I advise anyone who utilizes channeled messages to listen to their heart. Does the message resonate with what they "feel" to be true?

I have found that people who have had a lot of interactions with extraterrestrial phenomenon, and/or have been involved with black ops or other secret programs, generally do not think highly of channeled information, because they are locked into that point of view. I am told that people of low energy communicate telepathically with dark entities, by using fear-producing techniques.

I see now that my earlier messages, that follow in this chapter, had been influenced by concepts from others, books I had read, movies, the media, plus the words I used in newsletters, presentations and radio interviews. Looking back on the messages in this chapter, from my current level of consciousness, I can see these influences, yet I believe the communications to be mostly accurate and to be of great value, as most of the information is in accord with what I now know. I believe my later channelings and automatic writing to be relatively free of distorting influences, because I now am at an even higher level of consciousness.

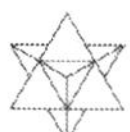

On September 23, 2008 I received my first communication from an extraterrestrial. I posted it at Mark's Corner. It was from **Justine,** who was aboard the starship Athabantian. **Bren-Ton**, a being of higher vibration also aboard Athabantian, next provided messages. **Moraine**, an extraterrestrial also aboard Athabantian, was next. **Adrial**, a Celestial, rounded out those who provided multiple messages that I posted at Mark's Corner.

Automatic writing is the name usually given to the process, by which I received and recorded the material in this chapter. My current understanding is that these messages were made possible due to the presence of the Andromedan starship *Athabantian*. Those aboard stepped down their 15th Dimension consciousness of Andromeda, so I might receive messages at my 4th Dimension level of consciousness. The imprinting from my many lifetimes in Andromeda facilitated this channeling process.

To view all 152 postings at "Mark's Corner," go to the initial posting of September 2008 at: **https://www.cosmicparadigm.com/2008/09/9-23-08-initial-posting/.** You may then page forward to read them all.

I am amazed at how well events have tracked most of the material in these messages, or should I say how insightful my extraterrestrial and Celestial friends were. By going to "Mark's Corner," you will find very accurate observations of humanity's current paradigm, as well as other insightful information.

As I reviewed these messages, I found them to be inspiring and direct, but with more details than I could possibly include in the pages of this book. After a difficult time, determining which of them to include and which to save for another time, I decided to summarize the most important points as follows. Hereafter, words in italics are the exact words of non-human communicators.

Please keep in mind that I offer these postings as a contrast with what I now know. By reviewing them, it will help you to see the significance of what I present in Part IV, as well as the difference in my level of consciousness from Part III. There are significant differences, including words, between these perspectives, differences that affect how we view ourselves, and why we are here.

The following are summaries of my communications, from 2008 to 2010:

• An armada of the starships, of our brothers and sisters from star systems of the light, is currently in orbit about Earth. At Earth's invitation, they have been supplying light, to enable her to recover from the affects of the dark energy. They are also here to assist humanity through its transformation. They see themselves, as our brothers and sisters, because their ancestors brought life to this planet.

• One million years ago Earth, was a pristine paradise. She volunteered to host an experiment in human evolution. Four races were brought from nearby star systems: black, yellow, white, and red. They were all volunteers. The idea behind this experiment was to blend these four races, meld them into a unique race combining the best aspects of each.

• As part of this Star Seed project, Pleiadians supplied the white race. Sirians seeded the dark-skinned race. Lyrans contributed the yellow race. Andromedans the red race. The races that seeded Earth were not primitive. They were placed somewhat apart so that they could establish themselves before beginning to interact. They knew of their origins, knew of the Creator, and were telepathic. They valued their direct connection to God. These civilizations lived in peace for a long time.

• When the dark energy separated from Creator, it did so in the name of individualizing itself from Oneness. The dark energy decided to pursue what it wanted for itself rather than cooperate with the rest of the cosmos. Once that idea was planted in that ancient oversoul, it was but a short journey to expressing itself in ways directly opposed to the light. It began to feed on the absence of light. It soon discovered that it could gain power over others, by diminishing the light within them. So began a relentless struggle by dark entities to distinguish themselves at any cost, regardless of consequences to others. This is a trademark, of those who mistakenly see their individual path separate from the whole. This then forms the basis for the rugged individuals of Earth, for acting alone versus acting in unity with others, and it forms the basis for greed.

• The dark energy descended onto this planet hundreds of thousands of years ago. It engulfed the planet and her inhabitants with fear, created chaos, and degraded Earth's human occupants. Some agents of this dark energy appeared as gods to the humans, setting up the structures of enslavement that are in force to this day. Our star brothers and sisters caution us, to recognize that these agents of the dark energy are very real, infecting all of our institutions, such as governments, media, and corporations.

• When the dark energy descended, there were many changes resulting from the fear that overwhelmed everything and everyone. It could most easily be seen in the animals. Where once all lived in harmony, there was now predator and prey. Earth's axis was tilted, so that she now had seasons, and her poles were shrouded in ice and snow. Earth's inhabitants were gripped in a state of fear; it changed their DNA, robbing them of the loving, peaceful attitude they had brought to the planet from afar.

• Earth was harnessed with an artificial satellite (moon), that tugged relentlessly at her waters and land. Its larger intent to control humanity.

• The dark energy placed an energy field around Earth that our beneficial brothers and sisters could not penetrate. The dark energy blanketed much of this sector of the universe, but none so completely as Earth.

• The contributing star civilizations were aghast at the destruction wrought by the dark energy on those they had seeded on Earth. They saw it devolve their cousins to the status of "primitives." Due to scrimmages between the forces of light and the forces of dark, the four star civilizations were forced to defend their home territory, leaving those they had seeded on Earth to fend for themselves.

• Extraterrestrials see us as enslaved by our current beliefs, institutions and traditions. We have been taught to compete with each other, to see each other as different, and to seek first our personal welfare. As a part of the transition, many people will choose to cling to their traditional beliefs. Only those who have turned their backs on the current paradigm will remain on Earth to become the leaders of a new civilization, and the caretakers of Earth when she is returned to her pristine state.

• Our brothers and sisters point out that all is energy. Our physical reality on Earth is among the slowest in the galaxy. Energy shifts are affecting our physical bodies. We are advised to view our surroundings as a stage upon which a grand drama is taking place, and savor our time here. They encourage us to adopt an attitude of loving observers to what surrounds us.

• ETs see our religions as a form of mind control. The belief about the flawed individual was injected into humanity by the dark energy many thousands of years ago. It is this belief that supports the structure of most religions. Some religions believe it is their duty to kill those of other religions, while practicing the pious beliefs of their own. Some religions rely on superstition and implanted ideas, not truth. Religious beliefs are one of the principle ways in which the dark energy ensnares humans.

• The impact of the appearance of our star brothers and sisters on religions will be most immediately felt, as they scramble to explain how to fit their antiquated belief systems into the reality of sentient life on distant planets, and in plain sight in your atmosphere. The fundamentalists of all religions will attempt to turn their appearance into a fearful event, claiming they are evil, and that this is the predicted end times.

• The most powerful positive force behind the current civilization on this planet is the Christ Energy that Jesus brought some 2,000 years ago. That energy of love, despite the twisted religion and aggressive colonizing that emerged, has slowly permeated all peoples of the planet, evolving all, until today the great armada of starships is finally able to assist the transition of Earth.

• Fear enters into the equation by making people who are fearful subservient, and willing to give up their rights as individuals. Fear establishes the need for structures. Fear conjures up the need to believe in something without experiencing it.

• Preparedness is what the squirrel does to prepare for winter. Caution is paying attention around heavy equipment that might injure you. Fear is different from preparedness or caution. Fear is that which grabs your gut. Fear is most likely caused by not knowing the truth about a situation. Fear is disabling, whereas precaution and preparedness are enabling.

• As the light of truth and love increases on Earth, so do the dark activities of the powerful, the wealthy and the religious fundamentalists. Observe the activities of the dark. Do not fight them, for to do so gives them power. Simply acknowledge these activities, and then concentrate on love and beauty manifesting itself.

• Embrace change, and you will be more at peace. Find your center and stand firm. Retain your balance for the sake of those around you. Discover who you really are, and why you are here at this moment, and in this place. Everyone, even those who are of the light, experiences their lives against a background of darkness, for that is Earth's current condition.

• Look at all that you have ingested from television, movies and books, from your religions and from your schools. Examine how others have circumscribed your lives, others who do not have your best interests at heart, and are operating from their self-interests. You have internalized their propaganda, to make you "feel" accepted and comfortable. Our messages are offering you truth, and asking that you internalize it, so that you will act in a different way, so that you will awaken to the larger picture, and so that you will welcome us as your brothers and sisters from the stars who come in peace.

• You interact with aspects of the your reality, but you do not create them, nor does your individuated soul create them. The reality around you is created from energy through the cooperation of the oversouls and other agents of God. You are the beneficiary of that creation, not its designer.

• There is a small minority of humans who are awakened to the light. There is another small minority who are acting entirely in their own self interests. The majority of people are asleep, leading their conventional lives, wishing for nothing more than to be left alone, unwilling to see the larger picture, loving conditionally, and unable to act for fear of change.

• The attention of an entire universe is directed toward Earth and the transition of her humans. Think higher, think broader, and think deeper than you have ever thought before. The wonders of the universe lay before you. Leave behind your conventional ways of believing and of thinking. Leave behind the comforts and institutions upon which you have come to depend. Think new, think revised, think, as with a blank sheet of paper, with a fresh canvas. Revise your thinking about what comes next. The new Earth, to which you are invited, is a wondrous place filled with new delights, new adventures, new ways of doing and thinking.

• The current lack of publicity about important events is not an indication of a lack thereof; in fact it may be quite the contrary. There are many things occurring on Earth that are receiving no media attention. This is being done purposely. The controlled media does not wish to give information about these changes during this most important moment.

• Observe how the wealthy are taking extraordinary salaries from their corporations and banks, regardless of whether these entities are performing well or not. They are getting what they can while a sleeping population provides the means. They, too, have foreknowledge and are preparing by building shelters and retreats. Politicians are staking out their territory. Tyrants are securing their fortresses. As the light of truth and love increases on your world, so do the dark activities of the powerful, the wealthy, and the religious.

• Regardless of what they are showing by their actions, each human of Earth, and each being in the universe, is a child of God, and thus are your brothers and sisters. Do not condemn them, for chances are you once lived the life that one of them is now living.

• As long as anyone is hungry for food or love, everyone on Earth is impacted. As long as any one of your human brothers and sisters does not embrace the light, this universe is impacted. This is the Oneness of all.

• Begin to see yourself as part of the universe. Begin to see the

Oneness in everything. Begin to treat everything and everyone in Oneness. Experiment. Explore. Open yourself to be a child of the universe. See all as your sisters and brothers, all of nature, and all in the universe as One. This is what is being asked of you. So, think expansive, embrace your wildest dreams, think light, and think love.

• Do not run from the chaos. Embrace it as a necessary step to the new civilization. You will come to realize that the old ways do not work, that the new ways are the only path through the chaos. From this realization a brilliant new civilization will be born. By adopting love for all, by seeing all as one, you will survive.

• Do not get trapped in the rhetoric of the media. There is a universe drama being played out, and you are at the center of it. There will be some dislocations as the final act of the drama takes place. New ways of knowing and acting will predominate; these will seem strange to you at first. You will interact with your space brothers and sisters. You do not fully grasp, nor could you, the tremendous significance of the drama that is being played around you.

• The most important thing you can do in this lifetime is to tend to your own light, setting an example for those who observe you. Live in the light, love your brothers and sisters, give an example of the highest way to conduct yourself. Pursue that for which you came into this life.

• A nation dedicated to looking after the individual desires of its people is not based in love. The U.S. is based in individual freedoms, not cooperation to achieve the best life for all people. Examine the founding documents carefully. They were drawn up by men to preserve individual freedoms, not the collective good.

• The mass of people are asleep. They do not sense the light, nor do they see the darkness. They merely sleep. Yet, inch-by-inch their lives are being transformed. At some time each will awaken to the realization that there is a new Earth being born, and each will be given the chance to accompany her, or not.

• The sleeping masses are asleep because they refuse to give up their individual self-centered points of view. Religions, popular culture, the media, and most Earth structures are based on separateness.

• When one of the facets of disclosure is fully revealed, say the presence of the armada of ships surrounding Earth, this will eventually open the gates to full disclosure of the role of the non-indigenous beings among you. This will in turn show the control by aliens of your governments, banks, corporations, religions and media. Then ordinary people will at last understand the extent of their enslavement.

• The more difficult part to accept is the presence of non-indigenous races, and the complicity of governments cooperating with them, in ways adversarial to the good of the ninety-nine percent majority. For at the heart of all that is wrong with Earth, and her human population, is meddling by certain extraterrestrial races that have infected the institutions and beliefs of mankind.

• In the 1950s there was an agreement between the government of the United States and a race of aliens who wished to experiment on human subjects. They traded technology for the right to perform biological experiments on ordinary humans, with an aim of improving their own biology. These experiments are at the root of the missing children and abduction phenomenon.

• Another aspect of disclosure is the infection of religions set up to worship extraterrestrials who had descended from the skies. Most of our current religions have some basis in these ancient beliefs.

• The technology received from alien races, plus the billions of dollars spent on their development, have resulted in secret military bases on the moon and on Mars. Alien technology is at the heart of projects such as HAARP, that seek to control human behavior by broadcasting frequencies to induce fear.

• The chemtrails that cloud the skies are not some sort of benevolent attempt to slow global warming or seed clouds to produce rain. They are filled with heavy metals and biological agents that have now infected all Earth-humans.

• Humans require the assistance of outsiders, who are here in large numbers to do that very thing. They are here as star seeds, who incarnated with this mission as part of their soul contracts. They are here as walk-ins, who have come as replacements for original souls. And they are here as benign shape-shifters. There are over a million of these beings actively promoting the welfare of humanity at this moment. They are working to awaken us to new ways of seeing and behaving.

• Make no mistake, the process of removing fear as a basis for your current civilization and replacing it with love, as the foundation for a new civilization, will be an arduous process. Stay the course, as we have described it to you. Prepare for the collapse of your manmade institutions. Observe the changes in your planet's weather. Note volcanic and earthquake activity. Stay alert to the energies coming at you from beyond your planet. Much is happening, much is at stake in your individual responses to the changes.

• All shifts of the planet will take place gradually, as they are within the control of your space brothers and sisters. See the energies changing, feel the changes in your bodies, and hold fast to the knowledge that all can and will be beautiful, joyous and loving after the time of transition. As events come to pass, it is most important that you view these happenings without involvement.

• Your planet is hollow like most planets in the universe. There is more life within other planets than on their surface. You have fellow beings within the hollow of Earth. They are of a frequency that can live within the Earth. They have a civilization that is much advanced from that which dwells on the surface.

• Many on this planet worship the moon, with monthly rituals and songs to its beauty. Yet, the truth is that the moon is an artificial satellite. It is a hollow sphere that was placed in orbit about the planet as an observation platform, as a convenient way-station for space travelers, and as a place from which to direct energies to Earth. She will be removed in the process of transforming Earth.

• Angry words, spoken against the controllers of mankind, provide them with more power. Each rally against a government strengthens the current regime, and the existing power structure. However, efforts of peaceful resistance, of non-compliance, strengthen the light in all. Each individual who focuses his or her light on individuals without light makes a difference. No one's effort is too insignificant. Each point of focused energy counts, and it does not require anyone to expose him or herself to ridicule or rejection. It is not necessary to stand before the crowd and speak out; it is only necessary to focus your individual energy on achieving the goal.

• Every planet, every star has a soul. Every particle, large or small, is directed by a consciousness that works in concert with the Creator's Laws.

• It is not enough that you wish for us to come and save you. That we cannot do, for it would merely set the stage for another enslavement. If you see us as saviors, then you will feel that you need to do nothing. We will not play that game. We seek cooperation from those on the planet's surface. We need your help to break the chains, to loosen the gates, and to dismantle the walls of tyranny that have enslaved you all.

• Some people believe that they understand what it is like to function at a higher density; many believe that they are already functioning in that way. You do not, nor can you completely comprehend what it is to function at the lighter densities until you have done it.

• Each of you has an obligation to care for the human body within which you are housed. It is not possible to teach others about health, unless you possess good health yourself. You cannot give love, unless you love yourself. You cannot respect others, unless you respect yourself. You will judge others until you no longer judge yourself. You cannot ask balance of others, unless you are yourself balanced. You cannot teach others what you do not know. You cannot show others a right way to live, unless you are living it yourself.

• Humans will continue to be present on the new Earth, basking in her higher frequencies. Indications of this are the myriad children being born with extraordinary facilities of awareness. These crystal or indigo children are the forerunners of the humans of the new Earth.

• You will notice major changes in your own body, as well as those of others, as physicality resonates with Earth's higher frequency. The more sensitive among you are already feeling changes in their bodies. All will be functioning from a place of love, everyone will be telepathic, and organizations will take on new dimensions among people who are functioning from Oneness.

• The process of transforming humans from carbon-based to crystalline can be a somewhat painful and disconcerting experience. The true nature of man, as a soul having a bodily experience, will be the basis of all, along with the truth about the elegance of man's soul.

• In the future, the truth about mankind's history on this planet will be unveiled. The truth about God and His universe will become apparent, with the appearance of our brothers and sisters from other star systems. There will be no disease caused by fear, stress, viruses, bacteria, or parasites; these are part of the 3rd dimension fear-based paradigm. There may be a need for doctors to attend to the occasional broken arm, but physical bodies will be universally healthy within Earth's new environment. The environmental problems caused by the burning of fossil fuels and mining for minerals and metals will be terminated. The transformation will be swift, occurring over the coming months.

• The basic idea we wish to convey is to assume an attitude of unconditional love. The closer you can approach that wondrous state, the higher will be your frequency. Walking in love, walking in the lighter vibrations is what it is all about. See the chaos for what it is, a fear-based lower frequency. See the chaos as part of the play that was specifically written for these moments. Stay detached, and see all as a wondrous unfolding for your learning. Be like a young tree that flexes in the wind, bend with the coming changes. You are witnessing these days the final phase of the tug-a-war between those who adhere to the dictates of the dark energy, and those who are of the light.

• Beliefs rule the actions of most humans because you are unable to see the truth of things, because you understand so little of your 3rd Dimension environment. This is not a criticism, it is a statement of the situation in which the human race on Earth finds itself. Those in power use beliefs to control others. A strong belief in your own ability will carry you through the difficult times ahead. Such a strong belief will set an example for others.

• Each soul that is currently incarnated in human form on planet Earth is a member of a soul group. These soul groups have been together for a long time, experiencing many, many reincarnations. Among the souls within the group, the roles may shift in each incarnation so that one time it might be father-son, or mother-daughter. The next time it might be son-mother, father-daughter, brother-sister, cousin, friend, or distant relative. Over the past thousand incarnations, all roles have been assumed, including dark and light, master and slave, gay and lesbian, perpetrator and victim, as well as angry and gentle. So it is today that most souls on this planet have experienced multiple lifetimes and are here for their final lifetime in this 3rd dimension.

• We see many souls who volunteered to come to Earth at this time, stuck in the allure of the 3rd dimension. The 3rd dimension can be quite comforting for those who are well placed to partake of its wealth, comfortable living, and pleasures of the flesh such as a plethora of foods, entertainment and companionship. Alcohol and drugs play a large part in convincing people that their lives are satisfying. The entertainment and the media play a role also. It is with great disappointment that I report that the vast majority of humans are unlikely to take advantage of this opportunity to ascend to higher frequencies. They will choose to remain in their comfort zones.

• After you have raised your frequency to the 4th dimension, after your existing structures and beliefs have disappeared, after the Earth shifts are completed, and your lives have been vastly changed, this is the moment when you will find yourselves in a love-dominated civilization. Shift from linear time to the "now." Old aches and pains will be gone. You will have perfect eyesight and hearing, and your touch will be extraordinarily sensitive. Your bodies will vibrate at a frequency that disease can no longer reside with them. Manage telepathy, for you will have this marvelous gift after the shift to the 4th dimension. It will be gradual as individuals change one at a time. There is no way out of the 3rd dimension except through transformation.

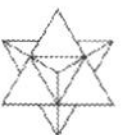

• **Yeshua (Jesus): The following is a compilation of his communications.**

Yeshua spoke about his mission to bring the Christed Energy to the humans of Earth. He had a natural childbirth and normal childhood. He gradually became aware of his mission. He traveled to other places like Rome, Egypt and Tibet. A knowingness about other inhabited planets helped him to love humans as his brothers and sisters.

Yeshua said that if you walk with Christ Energy, you will assume a new gentleness, a new tolerance, a new way of moving within a group, and a new friendliness. The Christ Light that he brought to this planet has done much to assist the development of our modern civilization. The Christ Energy is not the exclusive purview of Christianity, which itself is a false set of beliefs, about him and his life on this planet.

Yeshua states that the Christ Energy transcends all beliefs. It is a powerful force for good. It is incapable of being contained by a particular sect or cult. He did not intend to establish a religion. He did not come here to die for our sins. He came here to plant the Christ Energy, period. The effects of the Christ Energy have been largely wiped from our historical records, so as to minimize the impact of the Christ Energy on the development of modern civilization.

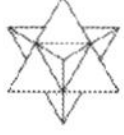

Rosio: In early 2009 I (Mark Kimmel) became quite sick. Every system in my body was affected from respiratory to intestinal to urinary to muscle/skeletal. I had a fever of 104, was unable to sleep or eat, and was delirious. *Rosio* was the Celestial who accompanied me through this.

My summary of Rosio's communication is as follows.

".... I am the Celestial who assisted Mark's body to cleanse and reconstruct to accommodate higher frequencies. It was necessary to remove an accumulation of dense energies that had built up over the past decades, some of them dating from childhood .... I am a specialist; this is my job.

"I wish to draw an analogy between what took place with Mark, and that which I see will take place with the humans of Earth. The cells of Mark's body form a symbiotic relationship with each other to fulfill bodily functions. Each is important, none unimportant. Each has a role to play. No one cell is more important than any other.

".... In the near future, my friends and colleagues among the Celestials, plus beings from other star systems, will perform for Earth and her people the same type of cleanse and replenishment operation as was done on Mark's body. Mark's mind and stability were sorely tested as this procedure was ongoing, thus will the collective mind of Earth humans and their stability be challenged ....

"Mark hallucinated. There will be wild visions and heightened energies surrounding Earth's transition. All will be affected; none will fail to notice that a huge change is taking place.

".... Mark will have a knowingness about certain things that comes from a close connection to those of us in the Celestial realm. He will see this as insight. It is a knowingness of the truth of certain things."

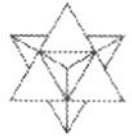

The following is from Bren-Ton:

"Welcome to Athabantian, a starship from Andromeda. This Galaxy, with over a trillion star systems, many of which contain planets nurturing various forms of sentient life, is the galaxy nearest your Milky Way Galaxy.

"Aboard Athabantian are quasi-physical beings whose planets have recently transitioned from the influence of the dark energy, plus beings who have progressed along the path of evolvement to where they no longer occupy any type of physical bodies, and Celestials from around the universe. All aboard Athabantian are at One with the God of this universe and the many other beings who are focused on the transformation of Earth and her humans. When I say we, I refer to the more than 7,900 Andromedans aboard this starship, not including the numerous Celestials and other beings aboard, plus those in the over one thousand other starships in this star system.

"Athabantian is a gigantic vessel many miles in diameter. She was materialized by the collective energies of over a million Andromedans working in harmony. Athabantian is a living being who communicates with everyone and everything on-board. Athabantian has free will; she volunteered for her current undertaking.

"Athabantian is currently positioned in orbit about your planet, but one quite different from that occupied by your communications satellites. When we lower our cloaking shield, you may glimpse us as a very bright object in the night sky.

"Our starship, along with some of us who are aboard, has been in your star system for over 70 years. Our major function has been to beam light and love energies to Earth, and to you, Earth's humans,

as you undergo your personal transformations. This is a cooperative endeavor along with many starships from around this universe.

"Enormous energies of light and love are provided. We, in turn, become receivers, broadcasters, and living examples of living in the light, and directing energies toward Earth. Thus, Athabantian, along with other star ships, became anchors for light and love. We are now seeking anchors among you, anchors who will perform a similar task for your brothers and sisters on the surface of your planet. It is necessary to have a high level of heart consciousness in order to anchor these energies of love and light.

"There are various (channeled) maps that predict the eventual shape of Earth's surface. Keep in mind that such communications are highly dependent on the background and dispositions of the person receiving the information. Thus, to arrive at images that can be communicated to others, the impressions from the higher realms must be translated by the receiver. Thus attempts to communicate how the surface of Earth will ultimately look are muddled. Plus no one knows exactly how a particular action will play out in physical form. If it is true of your actions, it is certainly true of something as complex as Earth's physical form.

"Eventually all humans who remain on Earth's 5th Dimension physical form will, of necessity, be functioning in the 5th Dimension – they will bring the 5th Dimension into their personal physical forms. Moving from the 4th Dimension density to the 5th Dimension density requires an individual choice on the part of each human. The infusion of the 5th Dimension into physical form is being accelerated by the efforts of numerous light workers as they give of themselves to assist Earth's return to a pristine condition and then her advancement to a brilliant self-illuminating globe. By doing this, they assist all to more easily make this transformation."

6

As I reviewed the material in the preceding chapter, I now see that the extraterrestrials and Celestials, who communicated with me at that time, were of a higher consciousness than was I. They communicated concepts to me that I turned into typed words, words that were influenced by what I had learned from other humans, my beliefs, and my background.

In contrast with my 4th Dimension perspective of 2008, my Cosmic Paradigm viewpoint, as of 2017, is quite different. It is not unlike the perspective of a fish as it tries to make sense of objects above the surface of the water (2008), compared to the broader vision of an eagle as it soars high above it all (2017). My eagle perspective of today would use different words to express the same concepts being communicated to me from the same beings. In other words, the messages would turn out differently. As I now look back at these earlier messages, I do not agree with all of them; I point out my differences below.

At the same time there are many threads that are similar, both in the material of the preceding chapter and in the chapters that follow. Almost all of what I have received is uplifting, coming from beings of Light and Love; I have had virtually no interaction with dark beings.

Communications, similar to those in the prior chapter, can be found in the channelings of others. For me, this is an indication that all were received by individuals functioning from similar levels of consciousness.

Please read this entire book before judging the words here and in the prior chapter. Also, you will find some terminology in Part IV to be different, from that used by my extraterrestrial friends in this Part III.

I recall a quiet urging to hurry up and finish my third book, *One,* because something new was about to happen. Not long thereafter, I remember the day quite clearly, when I was standing next to our refrigerator in the kitchen of our home in Fort Collins, Colorado. A telepathic voice said, quite directly, "We want to give you some communications, and we want you to post them on your web site."

Startled by the clarity of the words, my immediate response was, "No way."

The next day, my response to the words was, "No. I don't want people to think I'm crazy."

It would be a few days until I felt that I was receiving the telepathic words of an extraterrestrial. I posted the first communication on September 23, 2008.

As I said earlier, I posted messages at *www.cosmicparadigm.com* under the name, "Mark's Corner," hoping that no one would find the messages. Of course, those who visited the web site did find the messages and spread the word.

As I write this book, I am still amazed that I am really communicating with non-humans, even though, as I recounted earlier, I have felt their energies in my physical body. At this moment, I feel their energies as I type these words. I now have one-on-one discussions with both Archangels and extraterrestrials. I have channeled them and nonphysicals before groups large and small. People who have witnessed this process tell me that they can see an aura about me and can tell that my body, voice and delivery change. I am very blessed for all that has happened to me since I began receiving these messages. I see in them how far I had advanced from my days as a businessman, and how far I had removed myself from my 3rd Dimension life.

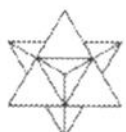

During the time of my early communications, **Moraine** said to me, "We found you." She went on to explain that she and **Justine** had been close friends of mine in my prior lifetime, that they had witnessed my interest in Earth's resurrection, had witnessed me voluntarily lay down my body, and knew that I had come into an Earth human body. They came to Earth aboard the starship Athabantian when it came to orbit Earth. Because of our historical imprint, they found that channeling to me was easy. At that time, my consciousness was barely open enough to recognize that **Justine, Moraine,** and I had lived together as friends. Only much later did I realize that it was in the Andromeda Galaxy.

Not included in the summaries in the prior chapter are the following topics that can be found at "Mark's Corner:"

- U.S. politics
- food and health issues
- wars, uprisings, altercations, and violence
- a different planet for sleeping humanity
- diseases
- global warming
- comparisons to other planets
- cleansing of Earth's environment
- Indigenous people
- new organizations — cooperatives
- leadership

The following are my comments about the messages in Chapter 6.

• According to information supplied to me by Archangels, the messages about benevolent extraterrestrials bringing their races to "seed" this planet with physical beings are not correct. First of all, these interactions took place after our primitive ancestors were created, 500,000 years ago, by non-physical beings, as a part of resurrecting Earth. They lived on Earth for some time in very primitive form. Second, there were no physical beings brought to Earth by beneficial extraterrestrials. Our star brothers and sisters brought energies, not physical beings. These energies were integrated into Earth's existing population, modifying the primitive physical beings. To believe that physical beings from other star systems were brought here is a 3rd Dimension way of seeing the energies that extraterrestrials brought. This is an important distinction when it comes to discovering the power of energies, and why we are here, as discussed in Part IV.

• After some time, there was agreement among the beneficial extraterrestrials who had brought energies to uplift primitive humanity, as to a single 3rd Dimension physical form for humans, but not in ways in which the different races of humans would think and behave. An imprinting from the contributing races remained with the different races of humans. It can be seen today by examining the differences in which individuals from the major human races think and believe. These upgraded races were primitive. They did not have the brain power to know their extraterrestrial linkage or have belief in a Creator. These things were left for them to discover.

• Later in ancient history, there were detrimental extraterrestrials who came to Earth in physical form, and who interacted with some of our primitive ancestors after they had already been upgraded by the energies from beneficial extraterrestrials. They enslaved some of these ancient humans, but not all, through biotechnology and other means. It is these detrimental extraterrestrials that are referenced in the Sumerian, Gnostic, Mesopotamian and Egyptian writings, along with stories about the Nibiru. Some of these extraterrestrials were regarded as gods, leading to early religions, with multiple deities. From my current perspective, I see that the investigators who examine these old records do so based on the 3rd Dimension, conventional paradigm. Some investigators and lightworkers call the civilizations described in ancient writings, Atlantis. This is mistakenly done without identifying marks that indeed these civilizations were Atlantis, or knowing the truth about Atlantian civilization. I will give my understanding of Atlantis in Part IV.

• As I will discuss in Part IV, dark beings, in which the light of Source is very minimal, came about in a way very different than that offered by the messages in the previous chapter. There was no single powerful dark force that separated from Creator. A dark force did not "engulf the planet and her inhabitants with fear, creating chaos, and degrading Earth's human occupants." I see beings that most people would call "dark" as those who are totally self-centered, and unwilling to consider the needs of others. Despite portrayals to the contrary, there are few beings so dark as to be considered "evil."

• There is not, and never was, an overwhelming dark force, rather there were, and still are, numbers of dark entities, as will be discussed in Part IV. Beliefs about a dark force overwhelming all of humanity have been promoted by dark beings, to mislead people about their influence, whereas their influence has been sporadic and limited to the control of individuals and, occasionally, nations.

Today the vast majority of humans are functioning at 4th Dimension, wherein fear is not the basis for every thought or action. In contrast with our planet, 99% of the beings in the entire physical universe are benevolent and of a high consciousness.

• I see dark beings acting to "distinguish themselves at any cost, regardless of consequences to others." Psychologists would call them psychopathic. I see that they have a powerful influence in certain instances. I agree with the statement of my extraterrestrial friends, that individuals of dark energy are "very real, infecting all of our institutions, such as governments, media, and corporations." I also see that activities of these dark entities form "the basis for the rugged individual of Earth, for acting alone versus seeing oneself in unity with others, thus forming the basis for greed." This is the opposite of beings acting from a basis of unconditional Love and perfect Unity.

• I have been told that dark beings came to Earth after our beneficial star brothers and sisters upgraded primitive humans. They enslaved some humans, but not all, through biotechnology and other means. I believe that some of them appeared as gods, creating primitive religions. They showed humans under their influence how to compete and dominate each other.

• The messages tell of a great battle between the dark and the light. I see this as 3rd Dimension thinking. Beings filled with the energy of Light, Love and Unity do not engage in contests, rather they envelop others in Love and Oneness.

• We see chemtrails, aerial spraying, in the skies overhead frequently. Many believe they are contrails left by passing jet aircraft. Evidence has shown they are different; chemtrails are just as our extraterrestrial friends have said: They are attempts at weather modification, and the substances are harmful to humans.

• There are references to a new civilization, as an extrapolation of our current one. I now understand that our ultimate goal is the restoration of Earth to a 12th Dimension Christed planet of Light, Love and Unity. When I wrote my book, *Birthing A New Civilization*, I was at a level of consciousness that put forth extrapolation. Now I see that focusing on extrapolations sidetracks our path to that ultimate goal.

• There is a trifurcation of humanity. Those who are awake to the Larger Picture, those who work to extend the current paradigm to continue, the status quo, and those who are asleep. All in the universe are called to be in unity with everything. Those who are asleep rule out unity by focusing only on their own lives, for to be in unity with all requires one to be aware of the lives of all, and take them into consideration. It may feel comfortable to focus only on one's needs, but that selfish orientation serves those who want the status quo to persist. Those who are awake observe the trifurcation from a universe perspective. As they practice perfect Unity with all, they live with unconditional Love for all, and they find real meaning for their lives.

• One message tells of starships that will take away all except those who are awake; those who remain will be "caretakers" of the new Earth. I do not see starships coming to rescue anyone. Our star brothers and sisters have said, repeatedly, that they will not come to "save us," and that it is our responsibility to create the new Earth.

• The entire issue of off-planet beings coming in a mass landing, whether to save us or to further imprison us, will not happen because for them it is a much better tactic to undertake either uplifting or depressing actions without fanfare. Beneficial extraterrestrials have been doing just that, so that we do not treat them as gods and embark on another round of enslavement. Detrimental extraterrestrials do not do it because it is so much more effective to corrupt our institutions and lower energy in individuals, and it does not lead to open rebellion against them. The latter do this very effectively by cleverly managing the media and other sources of information and energy. To my way of seeing it, the dark entities are being quite successful.

• The postings indicate that we should expect a significant event in the near future, such as starships appearing in Earth's atmosphere. Many see the fearful impact of that momentous event. Others await the coming of ships to rescue them from the planet. It has been over eight years since this posting, and others like it; nothing has happened. In contrast to this, I see a steady uplifting of humanity, due to beneficial energies and the work of wayshowers.

• Several messages spoke to near-term events such as earth shifts, destruction of institutions, and the appearance of our star brothers and sisters. They projected difficult times ahead, and advised survivalist-like preparations. I formerly bought into this, and acted upon it. I do not now ascribe to a survivalist mentality, for the worst that could happen is that I could die. I now understand that many lifetimes lay before me.

• I see disclosure as a slippery slope, for it will uncover the truth about humans who are working with off-planet beings, against the greater benefit of humanity. These humans will resist, distort, or lie about full disclosure to the bitter end.

• The moon is an artificial satellite. It's rocks are older than those of Earth. It is hollow, as shown in experiments conducted by NASA. I have a video, Moon Rising. Its photos of the moon's surface, made during a mapping of the moon by the United States Geological Service, show vivid colors, structures, and many saucer-shaped craft, all on the moon's surface. Now that I understand the true nature of the moon, I have little interest in ceremonies built around her.

• The moon was towed into place by non-human entities who wished to use it as an observation post, and a control mechanism over Earth and her people. I have been shown a vision of the moon being broken into three pieces and removed.

• There is a human base on the far side of the moon. This has come from testimony of humans who have been there. Pictures of it have been kept secret.

• The whales and dolphins are high consciousness beings, dedicated to uplifting humanity and the planet's energy. They were brought to Earth by the Sirians, rather than being the result of evolution on this planet.

• The messages about religion ring true. Fundamentalists of every religion judge those who do not believe as they do, marginalizing them, even to the point of killing non-believers. In past times, it was the Knights Templar who killed non-believers. Today it is the jihadists, who pray one hour and kill the next. Christianity has warped the Christ Energy seeded by Jesus; no longer is it based on unconditional Love and perfect Unity.

• The basis of capitalism is the energies of greed, domination and self-centeredness. There is no Love or Unity expressed within its creed.

• I do not see technology as the ultimate avenue to the positive advancement of humanity. As a venture capitalist, I lived on the cutting edge of technology and touted its benefits. Now I see that humanity must go beyond extrapolating new and better technologies. I see the road forward as an advance to higher states of consciousness, where technology based on the physics, biology and software of 3rd Dimension, and extrapolations thereof, will no longer be needed. I do believe that technology will have some place as we transition to this higher state of consciousness, but it is not the end game.

• Unconditional Love and perfect Unity have no place in conventional science. I see scientists attempting to extend scientific frontiers with quantum science and string theory to explain spirituality. I see new developments that come from a 3rd Dimension perspective falling short of what I have learned about the Cosmic Paradigm.

• Unity is different than Oneness. The Unity I have experienced shows me that everything is conscious, everything, and everywhere, even grass and rocks. Unity generally applies to unity with other conscious beings. I see consciousness in all things, living or not, when I no longer engage in the practice of "catch and release" when fishing.

• There are millions of higher dimension beings who live beneath the surface of Earth. I will discuss this more in Part IV. Scientists, and others of lower consciousness, who seek to find inner Earth civilizations, do so from their lower level of consciousness, failing to recognize how energy plays a role for beings who live within the Earth. When I saw the ET craft emerge from the side of the mountain, I was shown how this was possible.

• I do not agree with the statement that we cannot fully grasp what is happening. It may have been true at the time that the message was written; however, from my current level of consciousness, I see a far grander picture than expressed in the messages in the prior chapter.

• I subscribe to the concept of "standing tall" as a loving observer, as our transformation out of 3rd Dimension unfolds. "Be in this world, but not of this world" is a favorite quote.

• The most consistent message of these communications was that the ascension of Earth and humanity was to occur near term, and was to be an extrapolation of conditions on the current

Earth. My understanding is quite different in that I see our future existence in a semi-physical 5th Dimension. I see the energy of Christ Consciousness transforming everyone, so that they think, speak and act from Love and Unity. This will completely change the way in which we see ourselves, and how we relate to others, by organizing, providing, and accomplishing for the good of all. It may take some time for all of humanity to reach this state of consciousness. However, each of us can push toward that goal by the way in which we think, speak and live.

• These postings talk about Earth's transformation beginning 70 years ago. My understanding is that it began 500,000 years ago, when the first humans were created and were set on a path to resurrect Earth to a planet of Light, Love and Unity. Humanity is receiving assistance toward this goal from extraterrestrials, Ascended Masters, and Archangels, as we absorb Christ Consciousness into ourselves and into the planet.

• I have been told that by writing books and posting messages that I have anchored certain truths in this dimension.

• At one time, I had believed that Justine and Moraine were old friends of mine, and that we all existed in physical bodies on a physical planet. I now understand that the Andromeda Galaxy resonates at the 15th Dimension, meaning that there are, at best, individual semi-physical bodies, and more likely gaseous forms in collectives. This illustrates how my perspective has changed. Thus, what I know today is that Justine and Moraine were expressed from that higher dimension, so that they conformed to my level of consciousness, so that I could receive messages from them.

• Athabantian does not require a shield, as this starship is at a much higher frequency, making her invisible from a 3rd Dimension perspective.

• I was most pleased with the words of Yeshua, or Jesus, his modern Christian name, as they came to me early in my postings. He did live upon this planet, in human form, some two thousand years ago. He did bring the Christed Energy to Earth. The Christ Consciousness, of which Yeshua speaks, is vast, filling the universe with Love, Unity, beauty, peace and harmony. He is far different from the Jesus Christ worshipped by religions. Those who are willing to join him are bringing Christ Consciousness to all of humanity.

• Early Christian communities lived in accord with the Christ Consciousness that Jesus brought. They practiced love and unity in their communities. Under Emperor Constantine, Christianity became the state religion of Rome, and fear and judgment crept in. Christianity moved away from unconditional Love and perfect Unity. It became a religion, with structure and dogma, and it judged others harshly. Despite this, Christed Energy has had a great impact on Earth's civilization over the last two thousand years. This energy is an integral ingredient in the projected resurrection of Earth to a 12th Dimension planet of Love and Light.

• At one point in my severe sickness, as described by Rosio, I said that if my higher power wanted me to continue with my work, then I needed to be cured immediately. The sickness completely disappeared two days later. A blood analysis, taken at the height of my illness, shocked the doctor to the extent that she wanted to begin an elaborate investigation to "identify my strange sickness." I declined, and since have largely depended on energy work to keep me healthy.

• I learned so much from these messages as they came to me one by one. There is no doubt that they raised my level of consciousness, as I came to understand that I was indeed communicating with non-humans, and came to accept the truth in their messages. I am very grateful to all who communicated with me in this way.

• I recognize that the messages from my extraterrestrial friends and others, as presented in the prior chapter, show a fairly consistent view of humanity, Earth, extraterrestrials, and the universe. **I now know that I could have, very easily, become stuck in this way of seeing things.** However, Adrial told me to enroll in a course of study that would guide me to a higher consciousness. In the next chapter, I will discuss the course Heidi and I chose.

IN SUMMARY: I continue to be in contact with people who know me from my older level of consciousness, such as the Transformation 2012 conference, or my life in Pagosa Springs, Fort Collins, Ridgway and Boulder. I see how I have now achieved a new consciousness, not that there was anything wrong with the old ways in which I lived. It is just an appreciation for where I am now, versus then.

Now, as I connect with my old friends, it seems like so long ago that I was resonating with what they believe. There is a certain nostalgia to it. It is sad to leave my former comfort zone, but then again I feel that I have no choice. I know there will be many more lifetimes with my friends from this one, more lifetimes at all levels of consciousness, and experiences I cannot imagine.

I see my years when I was delving into the reality of extraterrestrials as a time when I was sampling everything but had no real center. I became convinced that we were going to create a new civilization any day. Heidi and I did not have a lot of money, particularly after she retired from teaching and we lost our life savings in a scam. We watched our expenses very carefully. We stored food and water to survive the pending transition due to the collapse of the government. We did not travel by air.

I became preoccupied with finding a "safe" place to live. This was based on statements from others, who saw calamity just around the corner with a government that was becoming dictatorial, an invasion by ETs who were not friendly, and scarcity of basic necessities. My friends reinforced the idea of the evil empire of the

U.S. My communications with my extraterrestrial friends could not steer me in another direction, because I was functioning from a lower level of consciousness.

Although I now see it as a time of fear-based thoughts, words and activities, the reality of extraterrestrials was an important part of my overall awakening. After my first week with CSETI, I became convinced of the reality of off-planet beings, and that they were here on our planet. This began my journey into higher consciousness.

In May of 2013, Adrial announced that she and my ET friends would no longer be sending me messages. I was heartbroken, as I had come to expect periodic communications. I received nothing more for many months. Then communications resumed.

The following is a telepathic message I recorded by automatic writing. Caltous is a Celestial, stationed aboard the starship Athabantian.

Good Morning, Caltous, thank you for responding to my request to discuss extraterrestrials.

Good Morning, Mark, I will be happy to undertake such a discussion with you. As you know I am currently a resident on the starship Athabantian, on which there are many so called extraterrestrials.

Let us begin by referencing energies of consciousness. The higher energies are based in Love and Unity. The lower energies do not have these characteristics. So it is relatively easy to discern two very different types of what you call extraterrestrials by examining their energies. From this, we can determine whether they function based in Love and Unity, or are based in fear.

You have designated them as beneficial and detrimental, Mark.

That is a good representation because those of the higher energies function from the basis of service to others. Those of the lower energies function from the basis of service to self, or self-centered.

Detrimental ETs express a dense body, or if you will, a physical body, somewhat like the physical body that you have. Beneficial ETs do not have physical bodies.

From an energetic viewpoint, benevolent ETs radiate the energy of Light, Love and Unity to all. Detrimental ETs have only a very minimal Creator's light within them, just enough to maintain life, and are unable to express any form of love or unity.

Caltous, are star systems either dark or light?

Good questions, Mark. As you have seen on your planet, those who function from the Light and those who have little of the light exist together, intermingling. The planets of a given star system are much the same within the array of planets, some will be predominately of the Light, some will not. On a given planet, it is almost always either one way or the other. Earth is an exception to this.

Please keep in mind that the vast majority of star systems and galaxies in this physical universe all function based on the Light and Love of Creator, and are in Unity with the All That Is. It is only in this segment of the Milky Way Galaxy that we find star systems and planets that do not.

You asked a question about detrimental ETs manifesting the energy of darkness. There are two aspects to this. First, those in whom the energy of Creator's Light burns dimly will appear to have darkness about them. They are wholly determined to seek only their own interests, without considering the greater good. So, to this extent they appear to be dark without Light.

Second, those without Creator's Light can actively manifest a dark energy. It is not just the absence of Light, it is an energy that they can transmit. I believe you encountered it one time, and found it to be very powerful. Dark energy is most commonly active at a subconscious level where humans will not feel it. It can be attached to seemingly neutral messages.

Just talking about this lowers my energy, Caltous.

Yes, it can be a very powerful force. So we will move on. Dwelling on it is the same as living in a state of fear, for most it is very uncomfortable.

ETs whose starships are of the Light will function beyond detection by humans or human instruments, because they are of a much higher frequency. The starship Athabantian is such a starship. It is present close to Earth, but it is not detected. There are other starships of high frequency also about Earth. The ETs aboard Athabantian are in unity to the extent they function as a collective consciousness.

Individual ETs from Athabantian walk on this planet, but are not seen by human eyes. You may "feel" their presence and you may communicate with them. It is possible for them to create a human body in which to function.

ETs also walk this planet who are without the Light of Creator. They have physical bodies of several types, such as you have seen representations thereof. They also have the technology to manifest very human-like bodies, particularly if their original physical manifestation would be shocking to humans.

One point I would add is the following. Those humans of different consciousness levels will perceive the whole subject of extraterrestrials or interact with an ET in a way consistent with their consciousness. Individuals with different levels of consciousness will see or perceive the same individual ET differently.

All of this is most interesting. Thank you.

Have we exhausted this topic for now, Mark?

Yes, Caltous, I believe we have. Thank you for this. I believe it will help many to understand better who and what ETs are all about.

Then I will leave you now. My blessings.

Blessing, Caltous

I will elaborate on the concepts expressed in this chapter, and much more in the chapters that follow.

PART IV

The Non-physical

7

The Cosmic Paradigm is a whole new way of seeing ourselves, our world, and our universe. It is understanding the non-physical as many times more vast than our physical universe, comprehending that light energy is the basis for everything, and knowing that love is the power that transforms light into form. Most importantly, it is understanding that we are Divine expressions in both physical form and in non-physical form.

I have acquired the material for this Part IV from several sources and in several ways. First, channeled messages from non-physical beings through Joan Walker. Second, interactive sessions with Archangels. Third, communications with extraterrestrials and nonphysicals in my quiet moments. Fourth, the guidance of Archangel Michael, as I type the words of this book.

In this Part IV, I will reveal the scope of the **Cosmic Paradigm:** How a group of humans, Ascended Masters and Archangels, including those from other star systems, plus the collective consciousness of Andromeda and beings of inner Earth, have formed a collaborative based on Christ Consciousness to transform humanity, and to place Earth firmly on the path to a 12th Dimension Christed planet of Light, Love, and Unity.

The material in this Part IV is, in some ways, a snapshot of my current understanding as events are currently in flux. Other material, herein, has a timeless quality to it, because it is part of the eternal cosmos.

Join with me as I reveal the various facets of this momentous transmutation, and how you can be an active participant in it. In doing so, I will answer four important questions:

Who am I?
Where do I come from?
Why am I here?
Where am I going?

All of this will help explain the energies that are flowing to this planet, and within you and me. They are the long-awaited transformation of humanity. The energies of Christ Consciousness are affecting our every thought, emotion, word and action.

There are no short answers or explanations to any of this, so bear with me while I unfold this exciting story. This is a journey of cosmic proportions beyond the confines of time and space. When I have done that, you will be able to know who you really are, and you will have real meaning in your life.

My current state of consciousness is the result of understanding and accepting the teachings of Archangels and Ascended Masters, and integrating the energetic templates supplied by them. I came to Earth with no history of the conventional paradigm. I see things differently than people who have had recent past lives on Earth.

I now receive messages from non-humans and nonphysicals in my heightened state of consciousness, and I can now say that I love myself. I now have a modest lifestyle, a wonderful wife, two great sons with their families, and friends from all levels of consciousness. Needless to say, I am happy and fulfilled, and most importantly, I have meaning for my life.

This is a whole new way of being for me, a whole new way to see the larger picture, to see myself. Having abandoned the cocoon of the conventional paradigm, I am now a beautiful butterfly living who I really am.

I am conveying this transformation to you, to show you that you, too, can walk tall while surrounded by the difficulties of living in a world of fear, anger, judgment and violence. That you, too, can achieve personal happiness and fulfillment, and that you, too, can find real meaning for your life.

My recently discovered status as a walk-in has filled in missing pieces of my journey. I now have a memory deciding to lay down my Andromedan body to incarnate on Earth. My presence within my human vehicle, a soul imprinted with the 15th Dimension consciousness of the Andromeda Galaxy, explains why I felt a restlessness to reach beyond during my years in the conventional paradigm. It explains why I did not apply myself to climbing the corporate ladder or seeking great wealth, according to the standards of that paradigm.

It also explains insights that I expressed as I went about life at that time, as well as the difficulties I had adjusting to my physical body. I was totally unfamiliar with life in dense physical form, because the last time I was on Earth was when both she and I were in semi-physical density.

Both Lord Metatron and Archangel Michael have confirmed that my soul exchange did occur. However, I have been unable to glimpse much about my prior life in Andromeda, because that Galaxy functions as a 15th Dimension collective, essentially energy with very little form. I do know that I had many lifetimes there.

I was living within the cocoon of the conventional paradigm, when they began my awakening in 1987. It took another nine years for me to turn my back on the business world. In another fourteen years I became the driver of my vehicle of physical form, and embarked upon the path for which I had come to Earth. Then it took another seven years for me to learn about being a walk-in.

I have also learned about "walk-outs." This happens when a soul advertises that it is ready to give up its human vehicle, one that has some good mileage left on it, and make way for a new soul to enter. To have a walk-in, you must have a walk-out. If the walk-out finds no soul to occupy the physical body, or if the physical body is not in shape to continue, death of the physical body results.

My two recent books, *Chrysalis* and *ICEBREAKERS,* were written after I had received information from nonphysicals, as disclosed in this Part IV. These two books bring in higher consciousness, Love, and Unity, all of which were not present in my earlier books.

Chrysalis, published in 2015, is non-fiction. It covers some of the information I had learned over my seven years with Mastering Alchemy and Seating the Divine Image. It pulls together, for the first time, angels and ETs to explain why we are here and where we are headed. Its contents are somewhat dated from new information presented in this book.

ICEBREAKERS, published in 2016, is in story form. Its setting is the Central Coast of California. The characters are: a well-known journalist who has published many exposés while working with whistleblowers; a woman with information about a secret program, telling him it will be the greatest story of his career; another woman in the hospital, recovering from her injuries due to a crashed ATV; and an unusual man,who helps her mend while discovering what she really is. The story line is that these four will soon become embroiled in a drama of galactic proportions, as they, with the help of extraterrestrials and celestials, unearth secret plans for the conquest of the galaxy. Woven into this story are components of the Cosmic Paradigm.

TEACHINGS OF HIGHER CONSCIOUSNESS:

As explained in Part II, I experienced a number of trainings leading to higher consciousness. The last seven years have been the pinnacle of my training, rounding out my evolution to know myself, as individual and collective expressions of the Divine.

Mastering Alchemy involves teachings, experiences and energy templates supplied by Archangels and Ascended Masters.

Cathy, a friend of ours from Matrix Energetics, mentioned a new course with Jim Self. After Heidi and I watched the 10-10-10 Conference, with Jim and Steve Rother on the Internet, we signed up for Mastering Alchemy.

MA's multi-year course involves studying and absorbing new material each week. It was there I was introduced to Archangels, as never before, and Ascended Masters, that I knew little about. Mastering Alchemy required daily attention to keep up with the voluminous materials provided. Each week was filled with exciting new discoveries. By the end of my five years with MA, I had acquired a lightbody plus other aspects of higher consciousness.

With MA, I began a path to the higher consciousness perspective of the Archangels and Ascended Masters. Before MA, I had focused on extraterrestrials to provide me with information beyond what I was receiving from other humans. MA took me to a whole new level of understanding. More importantly, I was now able to experience the non-physical under the guidance of the Archangels and Ascended Masters. Then there was work on eliminating unwanted energies from my bodies, both physical and non-physical.

During my time with MA, there was never any mention of extraterrestrials. Nor was there any reference to the highly conscious beings living beneath the surface of Earth.

During our years with MA, Heidi and I lived in Pagosa Springs, Colorado. In early 2016, we moved to the central coast of California. Now I am walking in three levels of consciousness: the 3rd Dimension for my everyday physical requirements, the 4th Dimension for interacting with the majority of my neighbors, the 5th Dimension for my interactions with nonphysicals, working on this book, and discussions with a few highly conscious people, local and via telephone and Skype.

Seating The Divine Image: In January of 2016, Heidi and I joined Joan Walker in "Seating The Divine Image." Most of those who are a part of this tightknit collective are graduates of MA. Joan had been a key part of MA, for she was the one who channeled the Archangels and Ascended Masters, for the entirety of my five years with MA.

Through the Archangels and Ascended Masters that Joan brings forth, I have now achieved greater levels of consciousness, further developed my lightbody, assisted my physical body to accommodate 5th Dimension, uncovered a personal relationship with Archangel Michael, discovered the imprinting of my soul from my prior life in Andromeda, and connected to Christ Consciousness. I can now say that I am truly an individual expression and a collective expression of the Divine, and an expression of Christ Consciousness.

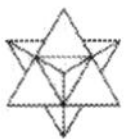

DEFINITIONS

Nonphysicals: Once the reality of extraterrestrials populating a vast universe entered my consciousness, all religious definitions of spiritual beings became obsolete. In this book, words like Archangel, Ascended Master, Creator God, and Source have cosmic meaning. This is much different than seeing them from an Earth-bound perspective. Thus, the Archangels with whom I communicate are great non-physical beings of the cosmos, quite different than the angels of religions. If that triggers a reaction in you, please bear with me as we explore these new perspectives, based on the Cosmic Paradigm.

My knowing is changing almost daily as I achieve higher levels of consciousness and fuller knowing of the Cosmic Paradigm. I see the limits of the dogma of the Catholic religion with which I grew up. I see the limits of the Urantia Book and other religions I have explored. These all are outdated by recent revelations provided to me by Archangels and Ascended Masters. I see traditional religions embracing elements of both fear and love in their dogma and practice, plus a belief in heaven and hell. I see them based on faith, beliefs provided by others, and written words from many years ago.

I now come from a place of knowing, knowing based on experiences. Nowhere in the revelations provided by the Archangels and Ascended Masters, or experiences with them, is there anything other than Divine unconditional Love and perfect unity. There definitely is no fear.

Christ Consciousness: It is boundless. It is transformative. It is a portion of infinite Source Energy. It is present throughout the universe. Christ Consciousness is the schematic of Source for creation in form. It is unconditional Love and perfect Unity, plus harmony, peace and beauty.

It was present in Earth's original creation, and remained on Earth until the Fall of Consciousness. Yeshua brought it back to seed it on Earth when he walked here. At that time humanity was not conscious enough to absorb but a portion of what he brought.

The Catholic Church and other Christian churches do not understand its cosmic implications, nor do they adhere to its teaching of unconditional Love and perfect Unity, particularly in their approach to those who are not members of their religion. Nevertheless, Christ Consciousness has had a significant impact on humanity's evolution over the past two thousand years.

Humanity has now evolved enough that it is possible to fully activate Christ Consciousness for the benefit of Earth and humanity. Recently a gigantic star tetrahedron of Christ Energy was placed in the core of our planet, but was not activated. It is currently being activated by the collective efforts of four groups of Christed

Consciousness beings: human wayshowers, beings of inner Earth, beings from three star systems and the Andromeda galaxy, plus Archangels and Ascended Masters. Thus, a grand collective, not an individual, will spearhead the second coming of Christ Consciousness.

Through the power of Christ Consciousness, all humanity will be uplifted from its current state of 3rd and 4th Dimension consciousness. This is the way in which all, regardless of their current circumstances, will move out of the conventional paradigm. All will awaken to higher ways of functioning that embrace Love and Unity, and, if they so choose, they will then apply this new consciousness in their lives.

It is now clear to me that I needed to experience contact with extraterrestrials, and receive messages from them, so that I might appreciate their higher consciousness and beneficial role in resurrecting Earth. (see Part III) I also needed to connect to and experience with Archangels and Ascended Masters for the same reason. Now Christed beings from four domains have come together to activate Christ Consciousness in order to transform humanity.

The following is a communication from Yeshua:

Christ Consciousness, Christ Energy, is present throughout this universe. Christ Consciousness is present in other star systems, in other galaxies. These star systems maintain their coherence in Light, Love, and Unity. Christ Consciousness carries with it the energies of Love, Light, and Unity, but it is much more; it is the energy of harmony, beauty, and peace. I have carried this energy to many planets in this universe. I carried this energy to your planet, Earth, some two thousand years ago.

I come to you today to give the blessing that comes with recognizing Christ Consciousness in your life. I wish to help those who read this book to understand what Christ Energy will do for them and for this planet.

Picture yourself as you were many years ago, Mark, as a businessman. At that time you did not see with the eyes of Love and Unity. You were operating from fear. Now picture yourself in the same business situation operating from Christ Energy. You would be seeking to help others on the basis of Love and Unity. All your decisions would be made, not on the basis of what they could do for you, but on the basis of the higher good for all concerned, employees, customers and shareholders. This would be quite a task as each represents different needs.

If you are in a place of Love, then you are serving the highest good of all. So you will first look at the needs of those for which you are supplying a product or service and fulfill that need. Then you will look to the needs of others. On this basis you may not have a viable company. So be it. If you are functioning at your highest, you may need to restructure, to find other ways to fulfill the needs of those who you formerly thought of as customers. Now they are your brothers and sisters, who are asking you to provide something. Find a way to give your brothers and sisters what it is that they need.

The others involved in your company will now behave differently. The workers will be here to assist you. The investors will, likewise, be invested in your company because they wish to assist you. This is happening because Christ Energy has entered the equation. Christ Energy has caused everyone to behave differently.

Now extend it to the time when all have advanced to the level of 5th Dimension. You no longer have a company, because your brothers and sisters can manifest what they desire. Yes desire, not need, for there are no longer needs. So you have no opportunity to have a company. It is not needed. When 5th Dimension is fully realized, your physical body will be filled with your lightbody, it will become semi-physical. It will be fluid. Yes, you will still be physical, but it will be a different kind of physicality. No longer will you measure things, as you did in the 3rd dimension. No longer will you have needs, or desires, for all will be available to you with little effort only requiring an intention.

This is where Christ Consciousness is leading humanity. Christ Consciousness is being dramatically increased to be infused in each and every human. Soon all will see others as their brothers and sisters. Soon all will operate from a place of harmony and peace.

Christed Energy is very infectious in a good sense. It will be within all very soon. It will remake your world. All will feel its effects. Christ Energy will enable Earth to once again become a 12th Dimension Christed planet of Love, Light, and Unity.

Do not concern yourself that you are not recording my message as would others to whom I speak. You are Mark. You are an individual being of Light. It is for this reason that I come to you this day. You write my words so that humans of a certain level of consciousness will read my words. Each has an individual contribution to make. You are making yours.

Dimensions: Before we move further into our journey to higher consciousness, I would like to say a few words about dimensions. You can learn more about dimensions by studying the golden age of Earth in the next chapter.

The physical stage upon which we all live our lives is commonly called 3rd Dimension, because we can measure height, width and length. It is a rigid platform caused by energy that has been slowed: E=mc2. Another way to look at it is: earth, air, water and fire. We live within it. We deal with on a daily basis. From this point forward, I will refer to it as **physical form.** I see it as the stage upon which we, the actors and actresses, play out our lives, rewriting the script when our higher consciousness so directs. In higher dimensions, we cannot measure height, width and length, because all is fluid.

Then there are the ways in which people live and interact with each other in physical form. If one is coming from a basis of overwhelming fear, then they are living in the rigidness of **3rd Dimension.** Along with fear, that grips one in the gut and overwhelms the possibility of higher conscious thoughts and actions, are the ancillaries of hate, judgment, greed, violence, and polarity. If you are living with any of these as the basis for your life, then you are living in the 3rd Dimension.

Those who live in 3rd Dimension believe that they do not have any choice because fear and its ancillary energies are so overwhelming. They act based upon those energies alone, dismissing alternatives. People who are functioning at 3rd Dimension are unaware that they are functioning at an unconscious level. They are, quite simply, unconscious that they are unconscious.

A higher level of functioning is **4th Dimension,** a transition between 3rd and 5th Dimensions. Here one is not consumed with fear; its associated attributes come and go. Here people have choice. Here they can see possibilities, and have the will and power to follow them, if they so choose. Ancillaries to the energy of fear, such as unworthiness, polarity, judgment and drama, remain in the 4th Dimension, but they are not as extreme as in the 3rd Dimension. Individuals can choose to rid themselves of these, replacing them with love-based attributes, as a way to advance to higher levels of 4th Dimension.

There are several levels of 4th Dimension, from fear at the lowest to love at the highest. Here fear is not overwhelming. Here love and its associated attributes can be the basis for thinking and acting, but unconditional Love is not experienced. The majority of humans live in 4th Dimension as they cycle between fear and love. In the past, I seldom lived with overwhelming fear, and never for long. Until recently I had not experienced unconditional love, I had lived most of my life in 4th Dimension.

5th Dimension is based on unconditional Love, of others, and, most importantly, of self, as well as perfect Unity with all. Unconditional love means just that: love without conditions. Unity here means seeing all other people and beings as brothers and sisters, all physical things as conscious, and knowing you are connected to all, both physical and non-physical. In the 5th Dimension, masculine and feminine are balanced within your body.

To stay in 5th Dimension requires one to master every thought, every emotion, every word, and every action at every moment. Many say they are in 5th Dimension; however, whenever they judge another, express anger, or feel fearful, they drop into 4th Dimension. In recent times, I have mastered living in 5th Dimension some of the time. I know when I slip from it, back into 4th Dimension. I observe others who claim to live in the 5th Dimension, yet when they express anger or fear, I know that they have slipped out of 5th Dimension. My experience is that it takes both intention and attention to live in the 5th Dimension.

My physical body has undergone many changes to accommodate the higher consciousness of 5th Dimension. The same can be said of my neurological system and my non-physical bodies. It has been a challenging road, and I believe I have a ways to go before I can maintain 5th Dimension at all times. I have a deeply imbedded desire to be fully functional in the 5th Dimension. I believe that a commitment is required for everyone who seeks it.

I do not believe that being in the 5th Dimension necessarily leads one to a pious life or the life of a monk. Carrying on with your normal everyday life, while remaining in 5th Dimension, demonstrates to others how they, too, can live in higher consciousness.

5th Dimension is the gateway to all higher levels of consciousness. In 5th Dimension, we have physical bodies with 5th Dimension consciousness integrated within. Once we move to 7th Dimension, we are non-physical, part of a vast realm that is many times greater than the physical. 6th Dimension is a transitional dimension, much like 4th Dimension.

12th Dimension consciousness is where Earth existed for billions of years. This is where she is headed as we resurrect her to her former glorious status. I do not understand what 12th Dimension is all about, other than the planet, and beings thereon, are in a gaseous state without form. Nor do I understand what it means that the Andromeda Galaxy is at the 15th Dimension.

Only in a physical body can one be truly an individual. Beings who are at 7th Dimension, and above, exist in **collectives** in the non-physical. The non-physical is many higher consciousness states for beings, like Ascended Masters, who have experienced life in physical bodies and have ascended. Beings, like Archangels, who have never had physical bodies, reside in collectives at 12th Dimension and above. Higher dimensional beings can express individual forms, not physical, outside the collective in which they reside.

I recall the first time my higher self was part of a non-physical collective. I was enveloped in warmth and softness without boundaries. Totally comfortable, I wanted to remain there forever. As I type these words, I can return to the feelings of that wonderful place.

I communicate with Archangel Michael, who expresses himself from the ultraterrestrial collective for the purpose of communicating with me one-on-one. I have channeled Archangel Uriel and Lord Metatron to audiences large and small. One time, Lord Metatron expressed himself for that purpose, projecting his energy in such unmistakable terms that he overloaded the sound system.

I am committed to further raising my consciousness. I am doing so, to be who I truly am. By broadcasting my energies of higher consciousness, I am assisting the transformation of this planet. This is the reason for which I came to Earth.

Levels of Consciousness: When I was functioning within the conventional paradigm, I saw everything in terms that could be explained from that level of understanding. My reality was formed by what others told me, and by my own limited experiences. I believed extraterrestrials to be science fiction. I accepted angels in terms of Catholic dogma. In other words, I saw from the perspective of the conventional consciousness, or the **conventional paradigm.**

When I learned the truth about extraterrestrials, the secret government, and the reverse engineering of ET craft, I saw everything much differently, my point-of-view was from the **larger picture.** When I then saw, from the larger picture, that much of the conventional consciousness was based on misrepresentations, my level of consciousness escalated.

I have now acquired a **Cosmic Paradigm** perspective due to my experiences with the Archangels and Ascended Masters. My level of consciousness has soared; I understand everything much differently than I did when I was functioning based on the larger picture, let alone the conventional paradigm. I do not see those who are functioning from those viewpoints as wrong; they do not have the advantage of my cosmic perspective. I can well imagine that as I transition to even higher dimensions, my perspective will once again change. I cannot even imagine the perspective of an Archangel.

One measure of achieving higher consciousness is the acquisition of a lightbody. Our physical bodies are being altered to accommodate 5th Dimension. Our cellular structure is changing. Some describe this as a crystalline body. I find the idea of crystalline too rigid; I like to think of my lightbody as fluid, completely integrated with the cells of my physical body.

I have found, now that I am functioning at a higher consciousness, that I can still relate to people of lower consciousness. My stint at lower consciousness undoubtedly assists me in this. Back when I was functioning at a lower consciousness, the things that people of higher consciousness expressed simply flew over my head.

Some in lower consciousness say that they seek to be fully human. Now that I understand the non-physical components of who I am, I honor my physicality. However, my higher consciousness self is the driver of my physical vehicle. I believe that striving for higher consciousness is the goal for which all should strive. Going one step further, living in higher consciousness, every day, every hour is the goal. By doing this, our energies assist all of humanity to the higher functioning of unconditional Love and perfect Unity.

Time: Physical time was created to assist 3rd Dimension beings to travel through Earth's rigid density. At the higher dimensions, linear time, as we know it, does not exist. The nonphysicals describe their time as the moment when things align simultaneously. Non-physicals "see" future events taking place at a moment of coincidence, not at a point of linear time. For past events, they see the events, but do not relate them to linear time. I can understand this at an intellectual level, but have a hard time incorporating it into my knowing.

In the next chapter there are sections that deal with the golden age of Earth. It took place over billions of years as we might understand time at this moment.

My friends tell me they feel time passing more quickly. I agree, as daily events, such as preparing to sleep, seem to occur more frequently.

Reincarnation: Oversouls are vast beings who have existed since the early moments of creation. They express individual souls, who incarnate in various bodies, physical and non-physical, to gain experience over many lifetimes.

This process is fundamental to the universe. It is through this mechanism that oversouls have many experiences, in different places, at different moments, and at different levels of consciousness.

In the case of the incarnation of an Earth human, a biological lineage and family situation is selected, suitable to what the soul wishes to experience. Often souls reincarnate with other souls with whom they have had other experiences. Often family members are familiar from previous incarnations. One incarnation may be as a son or daughter, the next a father or mother. One incarnation may be in a male body, the next female. Different races, different sexual orientations, different ethnic groups, and different socioeconomic strata are all part of the mix designed to provide experiences and growth of the soul.

Most incarnations are undertaken by means of a normal birth process and maturation. Others are done as walk-ins wherein a resident soul vacates a physical body, making room for a different soul. At one time, I believed that this process involved a traumatic experience, now I believe it occurs quite often and without trauma.

I had a vision, supplied by Archangel Michael, of a large tapestry with thousands of points of light at the intersection of individual threads. He said that this represented my many lifetimes, past and future. He pointed to one particular point of light, saying that it was my current lifetime. My understanding is that this is the case with all beings of form, including those on Earth at this time. All have had many lifetimes, on many different planets of this physical universe.

Recently, I learned the startling truth about my soul exchange, and am now able to vaguely glimpse some of my prior life in Andromeda. I now see my life, as Mark Kimmel, a human of Earth in a whole new light. After spending the last 20 years awake to the reality of extraterrestrials and nonphysicals, I have accumulated a wide range of knowing, and undertaken many extraordinary experiences.

I am just beginning to understand the ramifications of a soul imprinted with 15th Dimension energies from a distant galaxy, functioning in a body engulfed in the 3rd Dimension. I now understand events and feelings, during my life in this physical body, from a whole new perspective, and perceive external events much differently. I know that I have quietly seated my 15th Dimension soul's imprint on this planet, as a focal point to anchor energies that are coming from Andromeda. I recognize the energies from Andromeda as very gentle. There are no energies of fear or dominance.

I have also come to know that I was present in Lemuria and Atlantis eons ago, when neither was in physical form, in the golden glorious times, and in the end times. So my oversoul holds those imprints.

Death: Once you see the cosmic perspective of reincarnation, death takes on a whole new meaning. Most humans treat death as the end of the only physical expression they will have, thus they fear the loss of their body. We are taught from a young age that we must die, and that it is not a good thing. Most people have a sense that something comes after death, but they fear death because they are not sure what comes next. We have elaborate ceremonies surrounding death. Cemeteries are filled with dead bodies, so they may be resurrected to have another lifetime after the second coming of Jesus. Understanding reincarnation lessens the fear of death.

Where modern health care is available, more money is spent keeping a person alive in the final months of their lives than the cumulative cost of all their previous health care expenses. Pharmaceutical companies are always among the most profitable; their advertisements encourage people to think about diseases and then ask their doctors for their products. News reports are filled with stories about tragic deaths and the death of famous people. Novels, plays and movies are based on the drama surrounding death. All of this contributes to the fear of death.

People believe in heaven, because they have been told about it, because it is part of their religion. Many live their lives as if their actions do not count, so they do not feel responsible for what they do. Others fear hell and live their lives in fear of damnation.

Think of death as you, a soul turning in a used vehicle. Think of death as freeing you to embark on another new adventure. Know that you experienced what you needed; this is why you came into this lifetime. Be grateful for this experience on planet Earth, for many other souls wished for this experience. Know that you volunteered to be here, at this time and place.

In 2011, Heidi and I were driving back to our home in Pagosa Springs from a conference in Phoenix, Arizona. One of the attendees had recommended that we stop at the Airport Vortex in Sedona.

We pulled into the tiny parking lot alongside the road to the Sedona airport. I walked over to the map of the area; it showed a number of hiking trails, amidst red rock formations. My finger was led to a trail up the side of a nearby hill.

As soon as I took my first step on that trail, a force grabbed the front of my body. It pulled me along the path to which my finger had pointed. I stumbled forward, almost losing my balance, as if tied to the end of a lariat. There was no way I could resist. The force was powerful and unrelenting.

After a quarter mile, the force abated. I was standing on a rocky hillside, looking down into a deep canyon. I stood there glued to the spot, wondering what came next. Then a very powerful voice said telepathically, "We just want you to know that all we have been telling you will come to pass."

I have returned to the Airport Vortex several times. Each time I feel a strong urge to overlook the deep valley where I received the message. I feel a connection to it. So far, I have received no additional messages. As I write these words, I am transported back to the red rocks and that deep valley.

In Summary: I have had exciting experiences, learned amazing things, and received wonderful gifts since my awakening began in 1987. Both my physical and non-physical bodies have changed.

I now know about the vast reality of other parts of creation, have experienced the vastness of my soul, and have communicated with the highest non-physical beings of this universe.

This revelation could not have unfolded until I found my way to the clarity of higher consciousness. I am most grateful for the physical and non-physical beings who have assisted me on my path to greater awareness and higher consciousness. These have culminated in both an understanding and a knowingness that I am so much more than my physical body, that I am a Divine essence in a physical body, while at the same time being a vast non-physical consciousness. Extraterrestrials and ultraterrestrials, lightworkers and mediums, and many human men and women assisted me on this unique journey. I am particularly grateful to Heidi, who has accompanied me on this journey for the last twenty-one years. She has grounded me, while providing encouragement, as I presented and wrote about what I have learned and what has been communicated to me.

As I see it now, my status as a walk-in with a soul, recently migrated from a much higher consciousness, has paved the way, so that I have been able to receive telepathic communications, and have a real appreciation for the Cosmic Paradigm. Then I look back at my life as a businessman and laugh, the contrast is so extreme. I am very happy to be who I now am.

8

The following revelations are extremely important because they present information that is quite different than what is commonly viewed regarding Earth and humanity's history. They explain why Earth, in the beginning long ago time, was called the "Jewel of the Universe," and why we, the humans of Earth are who we are.

Much of the information in this and the following chapters is from Archangels, Ascended Masters and other Great Beings of Light. Some of the information came through Joan Walker, as an intermediary for Archangel Michael, and some came directly to me. The communications I present in italics are direct quotations from the source indicated.

The words hereafter do not do justice to the grand concepts I am presenting, but they are the best I have.

Non-Form: In the beginning there was no form to anything, just infinity in all ways. No shape. No colors. No sounds. No density. Only vast Non-Form existed, for there is no time or space in Non-Form. There were no swirling gases and no infinitely small particles. There was no form, or anything for which there could be form.

Non-Form is the infinite energies of Light, Love, Power, Consciousness, and Knowledge. Non-Form is not a point in space. Non-Form is infinitely vast, much vaster than any creation that flows from It. Non-Form is everywhere. Non-Form is eternal. Other names for this vast infinity are "All There Is," "Prime Creator," and "Source." Non-Form is pure Spirit. Spirit is Non-Form. Do not allow my use of these words to denote any limits to the unlimitedness of Non-Form. I do not use the word, "Creator," to denote Non-Form, although I did use it earlier to transcribe messages from extraterrestrials in Part III – when I did not have the understanding I now have.

This definition of Source is quite different from traditional religious definitions of God, who see Him or Her as an individual being, as a point from which all flows.

Non-Form is not a God that was created by human minds to explain the movement of the sun or the tides. Non-Form is not a God to whom one prays to end a plague, for rain to end a drought, or to control the eruption of a volcano. Non-Form is not a God to be feared, for Non-Form is infinite unconditional Love.

Non-Form is not some anthropomorphic creation of the human mind, to provide order to the chaos of the world. Non-Form is not an extraterrestrial, who wishes to be worshipped as a god in order to control humanity. Non-Form is not the God who created Adam and Eve. Non-Form is not a philosophical concept, nor can it be reduced to a mathematical equation. Non-Form is much, much more than the God of this single planet. Non-Form is a vastness beyond comprehension, eternal and infinite.

If you seek God from a traditional religious definition, and then project that to a God of the universe, you wind up with a conclusion limited by your traditional understanding. If you look from the perspective of the Archangels, you arrive at a completely different conclusion: Non-Form.

My extraterrestrial friends had been trying to tell me this, as they kept saying that they did not "believe" in God, rather they "knew" God. I did not get it at the time, because my lower consciousness was stuck on traditional concepts of God. If I were to receive similar communications from them today, I would receive them in light of the information in this chapter.

Early Earth: Non-Form determined that It wished to create individual expressions apart from Itself. These expressions were not to be separate, they were to be individual. They were to exhibit various unique expressions of Source Energy.

In the first wave of creation, in the beginning times, Earth was created as a gaseous spherical formation of light, sound and color. Great Beings, those that were very close to Source, undertook this creation. There were a total of twelve creations of this type, throughout the realm of creation, all were designed to allow the experience of individual expression. This occurred long before time and space.

Great Beings close to Source then came into Earth's spherical configuration to experience individuality and creativity in unique ways. There were no frequency ranges at that time, no dimensions.

Earth's radiance at that time was so intense that we would call it a "star." This was the beginning of Earth's golden age. It continued for billions of years.

Source Schematic: To create in form, **Creator Agents** were created by Source as unique expressions of Itself. They were given a schematic, an energetic formula, to follow in their creations. Today we call this schematic "Christ Energy." The Creator Agents were to use the schematic in ways allied with each of their individual expressions, in order to create uniquely.

(Note: The terms "Creator Gods" or "Elohim" have been used by others and by myself. The material presented here is so different from that found elsewhere that I wanted distinctive words, "Creator Agents," to designate these very special and powerful expressions of Source.)

The physical universe as we see it today is the result of the activities of the Creator Agents. The creation of galaxies, stars, and planets took place over billions of years. All of this was done according to the schematic of Source.

Great Oversouls were created to allow Source to experience individual beings in physical form. Oversouls express souls for each individual being for an incarnation.

Archangels were created to oversee this vast physical creation to insure that creations were taking place in perfection according to the schematic of Source.

To create physical form, Creator Agents use the energy of Love to compress the undifferentiated Light of Source, thereby creating planets, star systems and galaxies. All of this was accomplished according to the schematic laid out by Source to create individuality. The creation of our universe, as we see it today, took many billions of years, and involved creations at different energy levels.

Creator Agents use a process known as "energetic constructs," wherein undifferentiated light waves are transformed into light particles, which in turn are used to create the basic building blocks of the universe of physical form.

The energy of Love is required to transform Light into physical form. Einstein formulated this as E=mc2. This process created billions of galaxies, with billions of star systems, with many planets in each system. For me, it explains the true meaning of Love as a very powerful energy. The love we feel for another person is but a tiny subset of this much larger and more powerful energy of Love.

To gain some appreciation of the vastness of the physical universe (physical form) compared to the vastness of Non-Form, look at the distances between star systems. These distances are measured in light years. The vastness of Source is somewhat like the great distances between stars, compared to the size of an individual planet. Then, look to the size of the entire physical universe. Recall these vast distances when we talk about your soul and the vast oversoul from which it was expressed.

Traditional creationism is focused on God's creation of Earth, as recorded four thousand years ago in the Book of Genesis. Many religious traditionalists adhere to words, such as found in the Bible. An opposing view of creation is offered by Darwin's theory of evolution. It would have us believe that humans have evolved from apes. Atheists, and those of a scientific orientation, hold this view. Both of these theories are limited, by focusing on the origin of life on Earth, without acknowledging life on the many other planets in the physical universe.

The fact that Earth existed before the creation of the Milky Way galaxy, and that it was relied on as a guide for the creation of other planets, points to its importance. Our great souls were present on Earth in semi-physical form at that distant time. Earth today no longer resembles its preeminent status during its golden era. All of this provides an alternative story of where we came from long ago, just how ancient are our souls, and just how special is our home planet.

Scientists call the beginning of creation the "big bang," because they are seeing from a 3rd Dimension point-of-view. The actions of the Creator Agents, who are great non-physical beings, did not begin at some unplanned instant, rather they were deliberate actions utilizing the energy of Love. Furthermore, Earth existed for billions of years before the Milky Way Galaxy was created.

I see a **Cosmic Paradigm** that is much grander than any of the traditional views that focus on the creation of Earth. What I presented above, answers the question of what was going on before this physical universe was created. There was no "big bang," rather our universe was a deliberate creation by the Creator Agents of Source, after Earth had existed for billions of years. As I said before, the Cosmic Paradigm comes from communications with Archangels, Ascended Masters, and other non-physical beings. As you will see below, the Creator Agents made full use of evolution, for Earth today is the result of a second beginning, wherein life was reintroduced at the cellular level 500 million years ago, and evolved to where it was suitable for the later introduction of humans.

I now have a completely revised view of Source and creation. I now have glimpses of the vastness of Non-Form, but am unable to fully comprehend It. I have a knowing about all of this from my higher state of consciousness. I also understand that functioning at my old 3rd and 4th Dimensions state of consciousness, I would have been unable to appreciate these revelations.

While still following the schematic, some of these early Creator Agents desired to create from a denser form of Light. Some of the resulting configurations into more dense Light did not work out and were drawn back into Source. Later Creator Agents undertook further experiments to create in energetically dense form. It was at this time that Earth took on a little more substance.

In order to sustain these creations in the energetic configurations, dimensions were created, according to the needs of the Creator Agents. The 12th Dimension of Beauty and Unity was created first. 11th Dimension was next as creations focused on lower density while still retaining the schematic of Source. A time sequence was created to help with the intensifying interest of the Creator Agents in creating in form. Each generation of Creator Agents became more intense about exploring matter. Keep in mind that what we are discussing here all took place in form that was not dense, rather it was gaseous.

Luminaries, original expressions of Source who were on Earth in that period, were holding Christ Consciousness for the planet. They had trouble maintaining their energies when the Creator Agents created in more dense form, and returned to Source when 12th Dimension was created.

There was a further decline in the dimensions as the Creator Agents continued to create in denseness. The energy of separation was introduced when some of the Creator Agents forgot the schematic and introduced separation into their creations.

During this time there were some success and some failures. The energies of the failures was not eliminated from the energy field of Earth, they were merely set aside. Given the power of this energy, some of it began to replicate itself in dense matter. New creations by the Creator Agents that were in alignment with the schematic were infected. By then the energy of Earth had dropped to 10th Dimension. The Creator Agents realized that they had diverted from the schematic, and worked to raise Earth's energy to 11th Dimension. This period of fluctuating densities, still part of Earth's golden era, continued for a long time.

The Luminaries returned in an attempt to reinforce the original schematic of Source, Christ Consciousness. However, they could not maintain their energies in the 11th Dimension, due to interference from the earlier miss-creations. Once again they returned to the Energy of Source.

Nonetheless, the Creator Agents continued to be very excited about exploring what matter was all about because they had never had the experience before. Some of the Creator Agents merged with their creations to experience matter in order to be better creators themselves. Some of these experiences were very inhibiting to their consciousness. These Creator Agents realized that they could not stay in matter because it would damage their ability to create according to the schematic.

The stabilization of Earth's frequency unraveled and the planet declined. For a long time it fluctuated between 10th Dimension and 12th Dimension. Eventually, Earth was stabilized at the 10th Dimension.

Meanwhile, other Creator Agents were creating planets and star systems in the Milky Way Galaxy. They required constant reference points from Earth to remember the schematic of Source, Christ Consciousness. They came to rely on Earth to help them remember Source's energetic formula and bring them back to center.

However, some Creator Agents did not follow the schematic of Source, choosing instead to create according to their own light without Christ Consciousness. They sought ways to express individuality in ever more dense physicality. Some of these attempts failed. Judging the results to be without long-term potential, the planets and their inhabitants were all destroyed. Other attempts were allowed to remain. These began to replicate themselves.

Despite the fluctuations, Earth continued as the prototype of creation in form. Beings of other planets looked to Earth to maintain the schematic of Source, Christ Consciousness. At that time, Earth was many times larger than she is today in her current rigid density. Beings who had never experienced form came to Earth to experience what it was like to live in form. This situation continued for a long time.

Some beings of form on Earth, along with Creator Agents, experimented with what it was like to create in even more dense form. This was not done with any intent other than exploration. However, it resulted in energies of the planet fluctuating between 12th Dimension and 10th Dimension.

During this period, a civilization known as *Lemuria* occupied a large area on one side of the semi-physical orb of Earth. Its inhabitants were aligned with Source schematic and manifested Christ Consciousness. Lemuria was a place of great beauty and harmony. It was visited by beings from outside Earth who wished to see a civilization based on the energy formula of Source.

Along with the Creator Agents who were active on Earth during this period, some of the beings of Lemuria experimented with moving energy into more dense form, but always within the schematic of Source. These explorations caused more fluctuations of planetary energy between the 12th and 10th Dimensions. Lemurians went through several stages accommodating themselves to these fluctuations.

During this same period, there was a planet known as *Atlantis,* where beings along with Creator Agents explored many creations in dense form. These experiments ultimately led to the destruction of their planet.

However, the beings of Atlantis wanted to maintain their individuality, so they asked the Creator Agents with whom they were working to take on form in 10th Dimension energy to allow them to follow the schematic of Source while they continued to create uniquely.

They looked to Earth as the ideal place where they could merge with Christ Energy in a more stable way and continue their efforts. The Atlantians settled on the other side of Earth. (Keep in mind that all of this was taking place in a gaseous state of physical form.)

After the Atlantians arrived on Earth, a period of peace persisted for hundreds of thousands of years. This was a beautiful and harmonious period with Lemuria on one side of Earth and Atlantis on the other.

The energies of both Lemuria and Atlantis fluctuated as explorations into denser form continued. Despite these explorations, Earth remained relatively stable at between 10th and 12th Dimensions. Thus, the golden era of Earth continued, and Earth remained a beacon for many other planets.

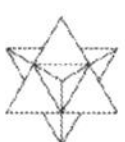

There are few stories about Lemuria and Atlantis when they were in semi-physical form. Most are about them in more recent times historically. What I am recounting here is what I have received from Archangel Michael, who observed Earth, Atlantis and Lemuria during this ancient time.

This era of Lemuria and Atlantis is what present humanity needs to remember. From the golden era of Earth we can glean that we are beings of Light who existed for many thousands of years in peace and harmony. Our fundamental nature is NOT in a constant struggle for the survival of our bodies. Our bodies do not represent who we are. Our bodies are only a way to express ourselves in matter. We have a choice as to what frequency range we wish to experience, which dimension.

The primary purpose of the golden age of Earth was to maintain Christ Consciousness and use it as beings navigated individual expressions in form. Earth's purpose was to bring into complete unity with Source all of the iterations of Source created in the Milky Way. This included both those created according to the schematic of Source and those created otherwise.

Many of us who are present on Earth today, as wayshowers and lightworkers, were present in Lemuria and Atlantis during this time. When the energies declined to 9th Dimension, we were unable to exist on Earth and left the planet.

We have now returned in human form to assist the transformation of Earth. At that long ago time, during the beautiful times of Lemuria and Atlantis, we each radiated Christ Energy. Wayshowers and lightworkers are now being called upon to remember those long ago incarnations, claim their Christ Consciousness, and broadcast it, thereby enabling the planet to once again be Earth Star, the Jewel of the Universe.

The residents of Lemuria and Atlantis were fascinated with more dense form than that in which they resided. They continued their explorations in conjunction with the Creator Agents associated with Earth. Some of these explorations resulted in miss-creations. The Creator Agents realized these creations were not beneficial, but they did not dismantle them. They were shunted to one side, coexisting along with the beneficial creations. The Creator Agents stopped using these dark schematics and went back to the original.

Nonetheless, interference came from the misaligned energies that were created by the Creator Agents as they sought various ways to explore dense matter. The denseness of matter led to separation. Separation led to the inability to maintain unity with Source. Earth fell into 8th and 9th Dimensions.

Separation led to the belief that one body type was better than another. This persisted as the energy of less-than and better-than surfaced. The denseness of multiple expressions created by the Creator Agents led to issues of survival and the energy of dominance-over manifested. This led to fighting among the beings of lower density.

This situation was repeated in other places in the Milky Way Galaxy. The original intention was to have Earth as a beacon for all in the galaxy, to demonstrate for other creations the original schematic of Source, Christ Consciousness. With the fall to lower levels of energy, new creations in other parts of the Galaxy had no example from which to draw.

On Earth, the Creator Agents did not know what to do. Beings from outside Earth who might help to raise up the situation did not come. They could not expose themselves to the low density of Earth's physical form, could not get trapped in it.

It was at that time that Christed Energy was removed from Earth. Imagine the impact of the energies of Love and Unity leaving with the Christed Energy.

The fall of Earth was precipitated by the miss-creations that the Creator Agents realized were not beneficial, but had not dismantled. They had been allowed to coexist with the beings who followed the schematic of Source. Although the Creator Agents stopped using their own schematic and went back to the original, interference came from the misaligned energies that they had created.

The Creator Agents now had an even more difficult time maintaining the stability of Earth. Eventually their experiments became so powerful that the stability of the entire planet was in jeopardy. When Earth's energy dropped to 7th Dimension, the Lemurians were no longer able to hold their civilization; it disappeared beneath what we now call the Pacific Ocean. Not long thereafter, the Atlantian civilization dropped to the center of the Earth.

Imagine entire continents disappearing, and the resulting impact on the planet. Imagine the huge distortions of the planet's energies.

Today, descendants of Lemuria live in inner Earth. They carry the imprint of the energies of Love and Unity that their ancient ancestors possessed. As their high priest, Adama, says (later in this chapter), they do not have a biological connection to the original Lemurians, because those beings were without dense physical form.

The energies of Earth continued to fall; it became more and more dense and shrunk in size. The only residuals we have of these civilizations are memories of their former inhabitants and the powerful imprint of the energies of separation and domination.

References to the "Fall of Man" reflect memories brought about by the residual energies of these events. Investigators have mistakenly labeled civilizations of only a few thousand years ago as Atlantis. What I have described took place a billion years ago.

The Great Catastrophe: Earth became a tightly compacted sphere of very low consciousness; it almost self-destructed. Non-physical beings placed it in a state of suspended animation until they could determine its future. No life forms remained within its solid rocks.

The Archangels call this event **"The Great Catastrophe"** or the **"Fall of Consciousness."** The destruction of the Jewel of the Universe impacted all in this universe, most particularly in this sector of the Milky Way Galaxy. It was as if a vital organ in a human body had died; the whole body was affected. Imagine the crushing disappointment in the nonphysicals who had observed the glorious Earth from her initiation billions of years before. Imagine the disappointment in those who had depended upon Earth as a model of Christ Consciousness. This loss was felt throughout the cosmos.

As we shall see, the lives of the current humans of Earth have been impacted in numerous ways by the Fall of Consciousness.

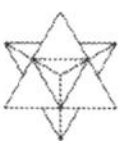

Some planets in this sector of the Milky Way galaxy had been so affected by the creations of the Creator Agents outside the Grand Plan that entire populations existed with only enough light to sustain life at 3rd Dimension density.

The Great Catastrophe also touched planets outside this sector of the Milky Way Galaxy, but their energies were only lightly impacted. These planets were able to retain unconditional Love and perfect Unity as their basis; these coherent star systems exist today at higher Dimensions in less physical form. Galaxies such as Andromeda were largely unaffected. Today it holds 15th Dimension consciousness.

Beings of the star systems of lower consciousness developed technologies that allowed them to travel to other star systems. There they spread living in 3rd Dimension as they conquered and colonized planets beyond their home. Keep in mind, these events began millions of years ago, while Earth was in its state of suspended animation.

Coherent star systems such as Arcturus, Pleiades and Sirius defended themselves against intrusions of beings without the Light of Source. Coherent star systems do not battle the dark civilizations, rather they hold fast to Love and Unity, overwhelming all with beneficial energies.

All of this was new information to me, previously I had accepted stories about Lemuria and Atlantis as occurring in more recent times, stories that others had told me, stories in books. I now see that some societies in the years since the rebirth of our planet absorbed the powerful energies of the original Atlantis of a billion years ago. The energies of separation and dominance have reemerged to enthrall humans who wished to control other humans. Off-planet dark beings, who have been involved with trying to control Earth, have made use of these energies.

The energy of separation causes us to see each other as distinct, and to value our freedom more than our connection to others. As a civilization we seldom act from the highest good for all.

I see the energy of domination present on Earth today, as we dominate the environment with pollution, mining, extracting oil, and toxic chemicals. We also dominate each other in wars, violence, and everyday confrontations. However, as we shall see, despite all of these negative influences humanity has struggled upward.

Archangel Michael has told me that memories of Lemuria, as well as its powerful energy, are manifested in the beings of inner Earth, who claim to be descendants of Lemuria. For me, these illustrations show that energies, both light and dark, are so much more powerful and persistent than I had ever imagined.

The concept of coherent star systems and planets embodying higher consciousness and Christed energy was also new to me. As we shall see later, this is an important concept for where Earth and her humans find themselves today.

The following is a communication from Adama, a high priest of the semi-physical highly conscious civilization that lives beneath

Mount Shasta in California:

Those of us who live in Telos observe your civilization from a unique point of view in that we are somewhat close to you both physically and in consciousness. We long for the day when your consciousness will rise to the point that we are able to walk among you, as the brothers and sisters who we are. Some members of humanity already interact with us, but it is by no means a large number. We would like to have a complete freedom to move among you. And it will be so, in just a short time now.

Let me give you our observation of your current situation, what you call the current paradigm.

We are well aware of the transmissions of your media. We observe that they are almost all based in fear, both the news and the programs. Your sporting events are based on domination, to a great extent. The news of the day is done from the most sensational, to appeal to the emotions of those who watch or listen. There is no mention of Love or Unity; no mention of the brotherhood or sisterhood of each human; and no mention of being in unity with not only each other, but with the planet. We see your media as an instrument of those who would control humanity for their own selfish reasons. And yes, there are those among the population who are aligned with non-humans, who seek to control all on the planet.

Despite this, we see there are some among you who are seeking higher consciousness. They base their lives in Love and Unity. These are providing the spark that will eventually transform all. We honor them.

You have asked that I explain about our connection to ancient Lemuria. As you know, that ancient civilization was based in 12th Dimension consciousness. It existed before the fall of consciousness, the great catastrophe.

We, who are of Telos, see ourselves descended from that ancient civilization, because we hold the energy of Lemuria within us. We do not have a biological lineage, because ancient Lemuria was not a physical civilization.

Our civilization of inner Earth came about in reaction to the invasion of Earth by self-centered beings from other star systems. We fled from them, seeking a place where we could develop our way of life without their interference. We developed the abilities necessary to live beneath the surface of the planet. There are many other planets that have similar civilizations, such as Venus and Mars. Under surface civilizations are quite common in other star systems of the Milky Way Galaxy.

Since the resurrection of Earth, the civilizations of Lemuria and Atlantis have again flourished on this planet. They arose because the energies connected to the ancient civilizations took hold among some of the people of the planet, and because visitors from other planets saw an opportunity to create colonies based on these energies. It is all related to energies, and how they manifest themselves in various forms. The energy of domination is the trademark of Atlantis, because it was that energy that led to the demise of the original Atlantis, and the near collapse of this planet. That energy is still present on Earth today in many forms, as humans seek to dominate what is natural of Earth, seek to dominate each other. We of Telos do not have that energy of domination; we have the energy of Love and Unity.

9

Resurrection: The nonphysicals placed what was left of the once beautiful Earth in a state of suspended animation as they wrestled with her fate. Earth was set to be returned to Source, where the planet would be regenerated in its original state. It was important that this happen so that the residual energies of separation and domination would not be replicated.

Sanat Kamura, a very evolved being from a distant galaxy, who was beyond dimensional frequency ranges, intervened. He was very proficient in the use of Christ Energy. He persuaded those who had placed Earth in suspended animation to set her on a course of resurrection, rather than returning the planet to Source and starting over.

An agreement including milestones was made to enable humans to evolve so that through their own efforts they might advance the planet out of the frequency of dense form. If these milestones were not met, then the planet would be returned to Source. There were no time sequences involved. Such a plan had never before been attempted. Since this long ago time, humanity has been able to pull itself up another notch toward this goal, sometimes at the last moment.

The lifeless orb of the former Earth was positioned to evolve through a series of stages to an environment into which they could later introduce physical beings who would eventually resurrect the planet with the power of their energies. So, about 500 million years ago, Earth began her long upward trek.

This distant beginning can be traced in geological records to what is called the Cambrian age, when trilobites first emerged. Geologists date these more distant rock structures of Earth back several billion years.

The nonphysicals wrestled with orbital instability and axis shifts as Earth's rigid body stabilized and was placed in orbit about the sun. These led to shifts in the tectonic plates; the incursion of oceans onto vast areas of the land, the rise, sinking and erosion of mountain ranges; floods and drought; extreme temperature fluctuations leading to ice ages; and then to global warming at the time of the dinosaurs.

The goal of Earth's resurrection is to return her to her former brilliance as a 12th Dimension Christed planet of Love and Unity. Starting with 3rd Dimension physical beings who would then purposely evolve into 12th Dimension Christed beings, and in turn, use their energies to evolve a planet to that same high level of consciousness.

We are engaged in the resurrection of Earth. The grandeur of the plan stirs something within me. I want to make my contribution to its successful conclusion. That is the reason I laid down my body in Andromeda and walked into a human body on Earth. It is also the reason many souls have volunteered to incarnate at this time and place.

Early Humans of Earth: With this plan of resurrection, our earliest ancestors were created by the nonphysicals and were introduced onto Earth about 500,000 years ago. They found here a veritable paradise, in rigid physical form. Here was everything they required for their daily lives.

Their immediate reaction was survival. This led to fear and all that came with it. It was the beginning of 3rd Dimension for human beings.

This is far different than the Bible's story of Adam and Eve. First, it took place 500,000 years ago. Second, it involved an entire race of beings, not a lonely couple. Third, our distant ancestors were very primitive. Fourth, this creation was done by Creator Agents, non-physicals beings working on behalf of Source, not the traditional God of Earth. Fifth, the stories in the Bible were written two to four thousand years ago; they were geared to a level of understanding of the people at that time. We now have a level of consciousness that enables people to grasp things much differently. Books like the Bible are relative newcomers; they arrived long after the original creation of mankind, hundreds of thousands of years ago. I assert that it is time to open ourselves to the more current information as supplied by Archangels.

This is also much different than the assertion that we somehow evolved from apes. Here we see non-physical beings using the undifferentiated Light and Love of Source to create in dense physical form. Here we see our distant ancestors with souls expressed from great oversouls. Apes do not have individuated souls.

The soul of our original ancestors was distanced from the body, because there was an energetic incompatibility between a low frequency physical form and a high consciousness soul. In these early humans, the ego was accentuated and charged with keeping the physical body safe. They had a minimal brain, just enough to function in their environment. The chakras associated with their bodies were largely dysfunctional. They had two strands of DNA.

I see many of these same characteristics in human beings of 3rd Dimension today. A fear-based level of survival is driving their thoughts, emotions, words and actions. Money and power are the ways in which they insulate themselves from knowing who they really are.

Although the environment was friendly, our distant ancestors were understandably insecure. They saw themselves as separate from one another, and spent most of their time foraging for food and searching for shelter. Fear was with them at all times. Their sole occupation was to live until death claimed their physical bodies.

They knew nothing about the larger picture of Earth or the universe, or why they were at a particular time and place.

I asked about the creation of the various races of humanity. **Archangel Michael supplied the following:**

After primitive man was created and placed upon this planet, it became obvious that humans would not evolve without some assistance from beings of other star systems.

We who had watched the development of early humanity saw this and approached the elders of two star systems, the Pleiadians and the Sirians. Keep in mind that the races of those two planets were coherent, in that they maintained their high consciousness and Christ Energy, despite the Great Catastrophe. Earlier they had benefitted from the example of Earth, as the Jewel of the Universe. We asked them to undertake the upgrading of the human population of Earth.

Using energetic technologies to interact with primitive human beings, they created two races of physical beings, the white race and the black race. This non-physical technology is beyond human knowledge at this time. They changed the basics of the human body, as well as the functioning of the brain, the neurological system, the glands, and the chakras. These two races little resemble what they are like today.

After some time had passed, it became apparent that further modifications to humanity were required. We nonphysicals then asked the Arcturians and the Andromedans to become involved. Using somewhat similar energetic technologies to create in physical form, two additional races of humanity were constructed. These became the ancestors of the yellow race and the red race. The fifth race grew out of the intermingling of these four races along with further energetic assistance. After a while, it was determined that a single human form would be selected for all races of humanity. This single form resembled current human form.

No one race is superior, none is inferior. Each race was given certain characteristics of mental and emotional makeup. Thus, you see people in different parts of your world thinking differently in addition to looking somewhat different. The long-term objective of these four races was a melding to create a blended race. The concept was never to create some sort of a super race.

All of this took place about four hundred thousand years ago. Since that time, there has been some blending of the races. One or more of each original race has touched all of the other original biological lines.

I understand that what I have presented is different than what has been circulated by others who received information from extra-terrestrial sources. The development of the races did not occur by physical mating of individuals from other planets with individuals of Earth. The beings from beneficial planets did not, and do not, possess physical bodies, such as lower consciousness humans of Earth would recognize.

The entire Galaxy of Andromeda functions at 15th Dimension and higher. As such, it is normally unable to interact directly with 3rd Dimension. Historically it has used the Arcturians, Pleiadians and Sirians to interact with Earth humans. This was true during the time of the creation of Earth's five races and remains so today. I am able to connect directly with Andromedan energy because of my imprinting due to my many lifetimes in that galaxy.

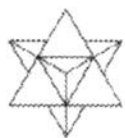

Beginning several hundred thousand years ago, physical

beings from planets with only minimal light visited Earth. These so-called dark beings had developed the technologies that enabled them to travel to other star systems, and to colonize other planets. They saw a planet with rich natural resources and a population that would be easy to dominate.

Some were hydrogen breathers, unable to function in Earth's oxygen-rich atmosphere. Rather than establishing colonies, they used biotechnology methods to create hybrid beings that could function in the atmosphere of Earth. They also have the ability to project very human-like appearances, they use this technology today.

Both beneficial and adversarial extraterrestrials have appeared in physical form, thus the origination of the gods of Greece and other ancient civilizations. Some beneficial, highly advanced extraterrestrials remained on Earth for some time, attempting to assist humanity. Unfortunately, they were all eventually overpowered, and memories of them erased by the lower consciousness, fear-based majority of the population.

Some of the detrimental or dark extraterrestrials enslaved humans to work, mining gold and other minerals for use on their home planets and in their starships. Zecharia Sitchin and other authors have discovered references to this in ancient writings. Imprints from this enslavement remain, to induce fear in humanity.

Along with influences by beings from other star systems, over the last 400,000 years, humanity has had to contend with volcanic activity, massive tsunamis that washed across the land, and extreme weather. The memory of these events remains to this day, fostering fears of Earth shifts and major disasters. This fear-based energy has influenced channeled information that predicts natural catastrophes and dramatic earth shifts.

500,000 Years Later: The human species has survived. It has evolved such that the majority of humanity lives beyond mere survival. There is a wide diversity of human conditions around the planet, ranging: from those in Scandinavia, who are judged to have the happiest lives; to those in Middle East refugee camps, who live with fear daily; from billionaire American elites, to the poorest laborers in Southeast Asian factories; from the educated in universities, to the uneducated in isolated tribes; from the spiritual in a Tibetan monastery, to drug addicts on the streets of a major city; and from the wealthy and powerful, to those who enjoy a simple lifestyle close to Gaia.

Most humans of Earth currently exist in the 4th Dimension. Gut wrenching fear is not a part of their lives. However, they do not practice unconditional Love and perfect Unity with all. The vast majority of people are comfortable in the lives they have chosen for themselves, be it wealthy, poor, spiritual, atheist, sick, healthy, or one of many other situations. Most are only vaguely aware of the background of secrets, manipulations, lies and disinformation that influences their lives. Most are unwilling to rock the cocoon in which they find themselves, or reach outside it for the larger picture.

Some are self-assured, believing that their lives are the best available, believing that they are somehow better than the less fortunate, failing to see each human being as a brother and sister. If the wealthy notice those who are poor, hungry or homeless, it is normally to give a financial contribution to some charity. They fail to see that whatever affects anyone on this planet affects all. It is unlikely that they will contribute to raising the consciousness of an entire planet. They fail to see the need to change.

As I wrote in Parts II and III, I hope this book will motivate those who sleep to understand that they came here for a reason. That reason is not to cower within the cocoon of family and comfort, believing this is just the way it is. You came here to assist in the resurrection of this planet to a 12th Dimension Christed planet of Love and Unity.

I have always had a feeling inside that I was no better than anyone else, even when I was living a luxurious life as a venture capitalist. I did not flaunt my position or wealth. I have not pushed others aside to get to the front of the line. I have not proselytized my vision or the messages I have received, rather I have depended on telling others what I know, and allowing my energy to influence those who are open. Despite my uncommon insights and messages from non-humans, I have never set out to be a guru. I am not sure where this comes from; I am comfortable telling my truth and letting others decide for themselves. As I explained earlier, I was never a good salesman, telling people what they wanted to hear. I am now involved in telling people what I have learned about the Cosmic Paradigm, not selling it, just telling about it.

In newspapers, television and Internet there is no mention of the larger picture of who we are. Nor are there references to the true nature of Love. Love is reserved for romance, loved-ones, or the ill or disabled.

On the other hand, there are plenty of references of fighting against some perceived evil, such as terrorism or drugs. Politicians do not take Love into consideration when enacting laws, nor do authorities when enforcing regulations.

The opposite of incorporating Love into our lives is fear and its ancillaries, in which much of the population of the United States lives today. People in a city of any size always lock their doors, even when they are in the house during daylight hours. Some have multiple locks on their doors. Where I live, in a more rural setting, we typically do not lock our doors during the day.

I recently visited a Post Office in a poorer neighborhood of a large city. The Post Office personnel were shielded behind bullet-proof glass. In contrast, the counter of the Post Office where I live is wide open, with no such bulletproof protection for postal workers.

To generalize for a moment, I believe it will be very difficult to convince anyone who is living a comfortable lifestyle to change the way they see life, to take the transformation of this planet seriously. It is very much like the 1% who give money to charity, never do they give enough to seriously impact their lifestyle. The status quo is so overwhelmingly comfortable, particularly here in the United States, that they see no reason to change, and will fight to keep what they have.

Yes, there are the starseeds and the walk-ins who see the larger picture, because they came to Earth with that knowing. And there are some with a spiritual understanding, not religious, who are focused on changing the status quo. These are the lightworkers and wayshowers; they are the exception to my generalizations.

I recall sitting in the lobby of the Hyatt Hotel in San Francisco some time after I had received my wake-up call, but while I was still working as a venture capitalist. I looked at all the beautiful people walking through that lobby and said to myself, "These are not the people who will transform this planet." At that time, I knew about transforming the planet only from an environmental sustainability perspective, believing what I had absorbed from others. I was totally unaware of higher consciousness. So, from where did that knowing come? I do not know, but I suspect it was my higher self making me aware. I certainly resonate with insights, such as this, today.

To get to here, from where we were 500,000 years ago, first of all, our species survived. Now, we are functioning at various levels of capability and, with the exception of nuclear war, our species is not in danger of disappearing.

Our current human species is the result of evolution. Each generation is smarter and better equipped than the previous one. Our brain has evolved, become larger and more flexible. Athletes achieve regularly better performance than in the year prior.

Some of our earlier evolution was assisted by the energies of beneficial extraterrestrials. We have received non-physical assistance, both energetic and from Ascended Masters, like Yeshua and Buddha, who have incarnated among us. We have received uplifting energy from the center of the universe, energy transformed by our sun and by beneficial ETs like those aboard *Athabantian.* And we have benefitted from technologies acquired from extraterrestrials, from agriculture to electronics.

In recorded history, there have been a number of events that demonstrate humanity's upward evolution. The civilizations of ancient Greece and Tibet demonstrate the emergence of thinking beyond the conventional. The Renaissance and the advanced civilization of China are further proof of humanity's evolution. The exploration of the Americas demonstrate how humanity reached outward to discover new frontiers.

At the same time, the actions of the Catholic Church show how those in power fear new ways of thinking and acting. I see great inconsistencies within Christianity. On the one hand it preaches love; on the other hand it exalts its followers to be warriors. On the one hand it sees everyone as a child of God; on the other hand it condemns those who do not believe as Christians.

In more recent times, democracy, as demonstrated by the United States, was a leap forward from the monarchies of Europe. The industrialization that followed led to a higher standard of living for many. The demise of slavery has been a giant step toward recognizing the equality of all humans. The same is true for women's rights, for the way in which a country treats women shows its level of consciousness. Our recognition that our environment affects all of us, and that all countries need to cooperate to deal with assaults on it, is a major step towards global cooperation. Properly applied, new technologies improve the lives of all.

The fall of the Berlin Wall signified the lessening of tensions between the Soviet Union and the U.S. The development and widespread use of the Internet and cell phones has transformed the lives of over half of the world's population. All in all, the majority of humanity has made major strides to setting aside the 3rd Dimension, becoming more conscious. I see these as very positive signs that we humans are slowly evolving to where we are ready to step into a higher consciousness way of behaving.

Many models of the new Earth are based on new technologies that will relieve people from the drudgery of repetitious work. Some are advocating that we prepare to move our civilization to other planets, as our own world will soon become uninhabitable. None of this thinking is based on Love and Unity.

There are groups around the planet made up of individuals who have discovered how powerful their energies are, and are now living at higher consciousness, radiating their energies to assist the resurrection of this planet. Some of these groups recognize the power of Christ Consciousness, and are working to infuse that energy.

As I have written the pages of this book, I have ignored, to a great extent, the programs and activities of the few 3rd Dimension humans and off-planet beings who are able to control the everyday environment of the majority of the humans of Earth. These form the backdrop against which all of us live, in most cases a secret and generally unrecognized backdrop. I refer you to Part II, where I have included a few pages on its many facets.

There are signs that the armor of the elites is rusting, that there are the proverbial holes in the dike. I see it in the grassroots political situation in the United States. I see it in international agreements on the environment, and the move to green technologies. I see it in the many new projects, primarily by young people, to create a sustainable environment. I see it in the openness of the Internet, as presentations of higher consciousness are made available to people around the world. I see it in the whistleblowers, who are brave enough to disclose secret information. And I see it in the smiles I receive, when I interact with someone who is straining to escape the conventional paradigm.

As I said earlier, the majority of humanity now lives in the 4th Dimension where visceral fear and its cousins are not the mainstay of life, where seething anger does not erode their daily lives. They cycle between love and fear, and sometimes they find peace and harmony, other times drama and fear. They enjoy their families and friends, and go about their daily lives without an agenda, without meaning to their life.

There is a very small percentage of people who are functioning in the 5th Dimension, at least part of the time, and more who are striving to obtain that level of consciousness. They have worked in any one of several ways to modify their bodies, their emotions, and their minds, to accommodate a higher way of life. They are spearheading the transformation to a more conscious way of life for all. They see that we may have some difficult moments ahead, but the outcome is assured.

The following is a quote from Lord Metatron:

You are seeing the disruption and upheaval that are necessary to bring about the changes that are needed so that you can create a reality that is truly based in Unity and Love.

Bren-Ton supplied the following:

I wish to comment today on your fear-based organizations and how they are collapsing in the face of Christed Energy.

Let us look at several examples: Your military is, obviously, based on fear. Your government fears the population so it enacts laws to control the people. Its police and other agencies enforce these laws. Capitalism is based on greed, a byproduct of fear. Your religions are based on fear, for they emphasize sin. Your medical system is all about fear for it focuses on things like flu and cancer, and keeping people from dying. There is little emphasis in the medical system on wellness. Many corporations offer products and services for protection and curing ills. Their structures are based on greed. There is no love expressed by them. Your schools do not teach love, rather they serve to reinforce the fear-based society in which you live. And lastly, your media is interested in the sensational, it most often reports some disaster or evil deed. You live in a society that has fear as a backdrop to your life.

At this time, the energy of Christ Consciousness is elevating all due to the efforts of many non-physical beings. This great collaboration, of which you have written, is destabilizing the fear-based institutions that under-pin your society. The structures are beginning to wobble as you can see in the dysfunction of your federal government. Governments around the world are being challenged by waves of immigrants. There is little love expressed by the actions of most governments.

It is important for you and other conscious people to hold to the concept of Unity. All humans are brothers and sisters. The way to higher consciousness lies with seeing all in unity and loving all. Coordinate with the Christ Consciousness, as it both elevates and de-stabilizes your institutions. Rely on your brothers and sisters. Show them love, your love that comes from higher consciousness, a love of acceptance of all in Unity.

There will be trying times ahead. Know that great beings are present to support you with their Love. Know that the Christ Consciousness is very powerful as it destabilizes your existing structures while offering you Love. Do not cling to the old; rather embrace a new way of living, in unconditional Love and perfect Unity. The fear-based structures that you have come to depend upon are going away. Find ways to live without them. Find ways to live at higher consciousness.

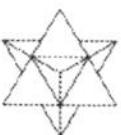

In Summary: From my perspective, I see that with the advent of higher consciousness for more and more people, many of the adverse activities of the wealthy and powerful are surfacing. One example of this is the domination of women by men in positions of power. Transparency of this and other issues is one key to the transformation of humanity and this planet.

I do not subscribe to the idea of an awakening based on new technologies, or better political solutions, or negotiated peace, or myriad half-way proposals. I do not see an extrapolation of our current paradigm resulting in 5th Dimension consciousness. I do not believe that we can rest on the shoulders of our achievements. As Einstein said, "You cannot solve any problem by using the same tools that created it in the first place."

What is needed is for individuals to recognize the role that anger and other issues play in their lives, to see how these affect their physical and mental health. Once they admit to this, then allowing higher consciousness into their lives will come easily.

A dramatically different approach is called for. What is needed is to give individuals a reason to move out of their comfort zones. What is needed is to show people a better way to live than what they are currently experiencing.

I have left behind my old life in the current paradigm, in the 3rd and 4th Dimensions. I know I am better for the decisions that have led to this. I rarely express anger at anyone or anything. I do not fear death, for I know who I really am: A great soul experiencing one lifetime out of thousands.

At the same time I do not judge others; everyone is free to pursue whatever path they choose. I can only wish that enough people do awaken, so that I may see 5th Dimension for all in my lifetime.

10

Physical Body: I have been affected by energies coming from non-human sources. They have uplifted my life dramatically, to where I can now say with a great degree of certainly that I am a physical and non-physical expression of the Divine, and that I am functioning with Christ Consciousness of Love and Unity. This is not a belief or faith. It is a knowing.

The 5th Dimension is the gateway to higher dimensions, higher consciousness, and higher functioning. There are a number of upgrades that a human body must undergo in order to accommodate 5th Dimension consciousness. Highly conscious wayshowers are now undergoing these changes, to make it easier for the rest of humanity to ascend to the 5th Dimension. This is one key to the process of resurrecting Earth to a 12th Dimension Christed planet, for in this transformation humanity must lead the way, albeit with the help of others. Let us now explore what is required to upgrade the human body to maintain 5th Dimension consciousness.

First of all, let me say that, as a direct result of taking these steps to remake it as a vessel for higher consciousness, my physical body is healthy in all important respects. I am able to maintain a reasonable weight while eating pretty much whatever I desire. I enjoy the taste of alcoholic beverages, but do not like their effect on my body, so I relegate them to food dishes. I exercise in concert with my body's requirements, and enjoy playing pickleball and walks on the beach with Heidi.

Beyond my physical body, I am composed of several non-physical bodies. The first layer surrounding my physical body is my **Etheric body.** In it are seven chakras: Root, Sacral, Solar Plexus, Heart, Throat, Third Eye and Crown. In primitive man, these were dysfunctional. As humanity has become more conscious, the chakras have become more functional. Full activation of these seven chakras is vital to achieve a body capable of holding the 5th Dimension. I can feel my chakras functioning differently.

My Root chakra, where the rational mind is located, no longer feels the need to take charge of my safety.

My creativity increased as my Sacral chakra was energized.

By enhancing my Solar Plexus chakra, I feel more peaceful, less prone to rise in anger.

I feel love, peace and tranquility in my Heart chakra, plus unity with all.

By activating my Throat chakra, I have become clearer in my writing and speaking, more open to speaking my truth.

Activating my Third Eye chakra has enabled my intuition to be more present. This chakra works in conjunction with my pineal gland to process undifferentiated light.

My Crown chakra is now open, to receive energies that flow from my seven non-physical chakras.

In addition to these seven major chakras, there are many more chakras in the etheric body. Two of these, the Sacred Heart and the Pineal, are particularly important. Both of these contain the flame of Source. These flames must become fully alive for the body to accommodate 5th Dimension consciousness.

The Pineal chakra, at the center of the head, is where the undifferentiated Light of Source can be brought and transformed into specific energies for use by the body.

The Sacred Heart chakra, located in the area of the thymus gland, but seated within the etheric body, functions as a center for receiving and activating non-physical templates. When it is functional, in additional to the flame of Source, it will hold the element of Love, and the Christed matrix. When a human is further evolved, the soul/spirit becomes seated in the Sacred Heart. Then the oversoul and the Christed oversoul descend into the Sacred Heart, along with the Holy Spirit.

Whenever I am troubled or out of sorts, or having trouble sleeping, I go to my Sacred Heart and review what a wonderful place it is. In a matter of a few moments, peacefulness descends over my body. I am smiling as I write these words, because the peacefulness of the Sacred Heart has manifested itself. I paused, just now, to allow it to flow over my body, clearing my mind and centering my energy.

There are seven non-physical chakras that lie above the Crown chakra. In them are portals to the Higher Mind, the Mind of Source, the Archangels, Ascended Masters and Creator Agents, and a portal to receive the Light of Source.

The **Emotional body** comes next. It is layered around the physical body. In order to remain in the 5th Dimension, one must clear it of all emotional baggage that has accumulated over the years.

Next comes the Mental body, a layer around the emotional body. Like the emotional body, it must be clear to hold the energies of Light, Love and Unity.

Clearing old negative habit patterns, all that is based in fear, anger, separation, less than, judgment and drama, must be completed to hold 5th Dimension. This is a process that may take some time and repeated efforts, but it must be done to clear the way to receive the energies of higher consciousness.

Beyond the mental and emotional bodies, we enter the arena of the non-physical. Here we encounter the unlimited nature of self, here is the connection to our non-physical collective.

An important aspect of changing myself to accommodate 5th

Dimension consciousness is to balance the Divine Feminine and Divine Masculine. These have nothing to do with body type, rather each brings with it certain characteristics, certain strengths.

Another important aspect is the remodeling of the glands to function in ways compatible with higher consciousness. Undifferentiated Light is transformed by the Pineal to reprogram the chemical and hormone output of the glands.

Then there are changes to the brain and neurologicalsystem. This is done in conjunction with templates supplied by the Archangels, and involve the Sacred Heart and Pineal.

Changes to the body's DNA are accomplished by directing this to take place. In my case, it was with guidance supplied by the Archangels along with Christ Energy. Additional strands of DNA, all non-physical, are put in place to enable 5th Dimension.

And then there is the creation of a merkaba. A multi-layered star tetrahedron of light surrounds the physical body. Its counter rotating fields provide a space of quiet and stillness. The merkaba enables one to travel wherever one wishes to go. This then brings up the axiatonal lines that interconnect all aspects of an individual to all in the cosmos.

When all of this is accomplished, the lightbody is integrated with the physical body, changing the carbon base to non-physical. The body's outward appearance remains the same, while seating 5th Dimension.

In my case, these changes are taking place in accordance with instruction supplied by the Archangels and Ascended Masters, requiring daily practice of meditation and remembering who I am.

I found this process uplifting in the extreme. I looked forward to receiving each new piece of information, even though I may not have immediately understood it.

I most willingly engaged in the recommended exercises. And I felt energetic templates, as they were placed in my body to upgrade my human form. Any time I am in the presence of the Archangels and Ascended Masters, I feel a very quiet but powerful energy, while in any moment I am not occupied with the day-to-days things of life.

I have found it most helpful to clear my energies at bedtime. I use the image of a red rose, a powerful agent of peace and power. I hold the rose about arm's length from my body, gather-in all the non-beneficial energies I have directed to others, and explode the rose to eliminate them. Then I use the rose to gather up all the energies that others have directed to me and similarly explode them away. This centers my energy and helps me to sleep more peacefully.

When I am feeling out of balance, I go to my Sacred Heart. There I find the flame of Source burning brightly, along with the element of Love, the Christed matrix, my soul/spirit, my oversoul, and the Holy Spirit. All have been integrated into my physical body, all assist me to maintain my 5th Dimension consciousness, all bring me to center. Now I know who I really am.

My higher mind shows me a clear distinction between thoughts, words, emotions and actions based in the 5th Dimension versus 3rd Dimension thoughts, words, emotions and actions. All is based on being a Christed Being of Light. A clear understanding of the 5th Dimension is required, and how completely different it is from the lower dimensions. There is a vast difference between talking about going to the 5th Dimension and experiencing the 5th Dimension.

There is a difference between viewing the larger picture from the vantage point of other humans and even ETs, and viewing the Cosmic Paradigm from the point of view of non-physical beings. In order to move into the 5th Dimension, not only must one's consciousness be changed, but one's physical body must be changed to seat the higher energies. In order to move humanity out of the 4th Dimension, its consciousness must evolve to a higher level.

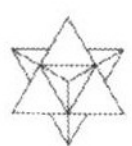

Soul/Spirit: In humans who reside in 4th Dimension

consciousness, their individualized soul is not integrated with their body, but lies apart from it. The soul designated for this lifetime is expressed from one's oversoul; it contains the many soul experiences that this vast and powerful being has had, will have, and is currently having. The records from each of our lifetimes that are important to the oversoul are stored in the Causal Body, another body associated with our human form.

Our oversouls predate time and space. Our individual souls are expressed from one of them for a life in an individual physical body.

The soul that originally incarnated in my physical human body was expressed by an oversoul. It made an agreement whereby it would relinquish my physical body at a certain moment to make way for me to come in, a soul exchange. I, the soul that currently occupies this body, has imprinting due to my many lifetimes in the 15th Dimension energy of the Andromeda Galaxy. My oversoul attached the imprinting of that 15th Dimension experience to me for this lifetime on Earth.

Periodically I have a vision from the perspective of a vast being who is viewing a tiny Earth from a great distance. I recall this vision quite clearly, and the feeling that accompanies it. My understanding of this is that I am looking from my soul's perspective as it views my tiny physical body. That huge soul now resides in my Sacred Heart. Since there is no time or space in the non-physical, this is entirely possible.

It is based on experiences like these, and information and experiences supplied by the Archangels, that I have come to understand that my soul/spirit is both vast and powerful. It is comprised of two parts, the soul expressed for this life and the spirit that knows no boundaries.

When I first learned of my status as a walk-in with 15th Dimension imprinting, I asked why I needed the discipline and experiences provided by Mastering Alchemy. I was informed that my rational mind was still too involved with my understanding of the larger picture, despite my uplifting contacts with extraterrestrials and celestials. Now that I am engaged with Joan Walker and the Seating of the Divine Image collective, I am pleased with the path I have followed, for it has led me to write this book disclosing my journey from 3rd Dimension to 5th and opening a door for others to follow. (Each time I write something like the above paragraph, I receive an energetic reinforcement that I have said something that is both true and important. My gratitude for when this takes place.)

Rational Mind and Higher Mind: Buried in the first chakra, my rational mind is a gift from those nonphysicals who created our physical bodies. When humanity was just beginning, one's ego was charged with keeping the physical body safe. As people became conscious, many saw it interfering with upward progress, so they determined to fight against it. Beings of higher consciousness recognize that to fight against something serves to strengthen it, so they make friends with the rational mind. Moving beyond fear is necessary to make this happen, for the ego feeds off the energy of fear. I can see others functioning from their rational minds when they demand scientific proof, want to analyze, or refuse to accept anything to do with the non-physical or beings from another star system.

When I am operating from my higher mind, I come from a place of peace and harmony. It is from my higher mind that I am writing this book. My higher mind is linked to the Mind of Source through my 8th chakra, a non-physical chakra that lies above my Crown chakra. I can feel when I am operating from my higher mind, because I recall what it was like to function from my rational mind. I can see others when they are functioning from their higher minds, as they are open to new ways of thinking, seeing and acting.

11

I see, very clearly, that the only way in which Earth can escape from its current paradigm of wars, violence, mass shootings, misinformation, secrets, lies, drama, fear, polarity, domination, greed and insecurity is by raising the consciousness of all of humanity. Anything short of this will eventually devolve to behaving in the old ways of the conventional paradigm.

I transcribed the following words from Archangel Michael:

To transform the energy of a planet, change the consciousness of its inhabitants.

The energy of the whole affects the energy of the individual.

The energy of the individual affects the energy of the whole.

The whole can be transformed by changing the energy of individuals one at a time.

It may take some time for all of Earth's humans to find their way to a 12th Dimension Christed planet. However, the journey to that ultimate goal is under way, despite what it may seem like to those in the middle of the tra[illegible]nation. We are in the midst of a huge increase in Christ Ener[illegible] am being told that this current infusion of Christ Energy will have a dramatic and immediate impact on all of humanity.

Already I see signs of a gradual awakening of people who previously were focused only on what was going on in their narrow lives. Now I watch as they notice that something unusual is under way with intense weather, wildfires, droughts, freezing and floods in unexpected places. The Internet brings to light the behavior of politicians, mass shootings, pedophiles, sexual abuse of women, false flags and information from whistleblowers, so that all can see the need for change.

If I focus on the disasters, lies and violence that the media exposes, I become quickly overwhelmed with negativity, and do not see a way through the chaos. On the other hand, if I take all that I am receiving from my extraterrestrial and non-physical friends, I see an end to the current paradigm.

With the infusion of Christ Consciousness, I know much will occur in my lifetime, and that my efforts, along with those of other wayshowers, are making it possible. We have but to reach a critical mass, then the rest of humanity will quickly ascend to higher consciousness. I have been told that the "hundredth monkey" phenomenon will come into play, at some point.

I know that I have touched the lives of many people, awakening them to the Cosmic Paradigm, helping them to see who they really are, and helping them to set aside the current paradigm. I have acted as an enlightened being of Light. I see this as my role, nothing more.

If I am successful in opening a door to higher consciousness for others, then I have fulfilled my mission in this lifetime, and my life has meaning. I appreciate the gratitude of those whom I have assisted.

As I write these words, I feel the love of those who have coached me along my path. I am very grateful to them for helping me to know who I really am.

I recently attended a high consciousness conference where I did not have a preview of events and did not know what to expect. To my astonishment and delight, the group of humans in attendance created a collective encompassing Elders of the Sirian Archangelic Confederation, Elders of the Collective Consciousness of the Pleiadian Star System, Elders of the Arcturian Collective, beings from inner Earth (Telosians, Lemurians, Luminaries and the Andara Collective), plus the Archangels and Ascended Masters with whom we had already been interacting. The collective energy from Andromeda was added to this.

My consciousness expanded to levels of which I had never dreamed. Much of my former beliefs about extraterrestrials and inner Earth beings have now taken a huge step upward. Never before, at other conferences featuring non-physical beings, had there been any mention of extraterrestrials. Mere mention of extraterrestrials, to the leaders of those other conferences, had been met with disdain. Now, extraterrestrials were vital participants in this collective of Christ Conscious beings, along with the great nonphysicals. I was stunned, to say the least. I was also gratified that, finally, the role of beneficial extraterrestrials was recognized by people attuned to the beauty and power of the non-physical. To my mind, this was an historic happening. This event has escalated my feeling that Earth and humanity will soon emerge into the 5th Dimension.

Later, Yeshua connected with the same group who had attended the conference. He spoke about seeding Christ Consciousness when he had been on Earth 2,000 years ago. Now he was returning to fully infuse it, along with all members of the collective who were present at the conference. A major step in transforming all humanity to 5th Dimension is under way, utilizing a collective of Christ Conscious beings to infuse Christ Energy into all humans.

I transcribed the following message in early 2018:

Good morning, Mark, it is I, Yeshua.

Good Morning, Yeshua.

Today I would like to give you a few words to include in your book.

That would be most appreciated and most appropriate.

The combined energies of those in the collective, as you have named them, will be extraordinarily powerful. They will be able to provide each human of Earth with the experience of living in Light, Love and Unity. Yes, I said the experience. ***Each person will have the actual experience in their lives of living in Light, Love and Unity.***

This is how it will come about: At the appointed moment, all in the collective will focus their energies on making this happen. Each human of Earth will awaken knowing that this day they can live in peace, harmony and beauty. Each will know that they can change their life to behave in this way, if they so choose. Each will be able think about this as they arise from their sleep.

This event will be true for everyone, regardless of their level of consciousness. It will be true for the soldier, the factory worker, the clerk at the store, the mother of young children, and the banker. The hobo and the soldier will know it. Each, in their own way, will see that it is now possible to lead a new life. Each will ask him- or herself, "Do I wish to lead my life in this new way?" Each will have a choice.

The experience will be very real. They will see their actions driven by the energy of Christ Consciousness.

This is very powerful, Yeshua.

Yes, Mark, it is indeed very powerful. And it will indeed take place as I have described.

I am honored to be receiving this message.

I encourage you to complete this book to assist people to more fully understand what is happening to them.

I most certainly will do that, and soon.

I leave you now, blessings.

Blessings, Yeshua

At this juncture, I think it is important to note: 1) Beneficial extraterrestrials changed our ancient ancestors using energy technology. 2) Yeshua is spearheading this return of Christ Energy, but he is utilizing a collective of other highly consciousness beings. 3) Humanity is now more advanced in that most humans reside at 4th Dimension, compared to when Yeshua introduced Christ Energy two thousand years ago.

I now see the path to the transformation of Earth and humanity. Christ Energy will infuse each person on the planet. It will cause each person to see life differently, to awaken to the possibility of a planet without wars, violence and domination. The very powerful Energy will startle everyone into seeing what their lives would be like based on Light, Love and Unity. Then each will make a decision on whether they wish to escalate to this new way to live, or continue with their old thoughts and behaviors. Those who do not choose higher consciousness will find it too uncomfortable to continue living on a highly conscious planet.

In that moment of infusion, the vision of a totally new way to live will overcome all other thoughts. The reality of a new way of being, based on Christ Energy of Love, Unity, peace, harmony and beauty, will overwhelm each individual. If they so choose, then each will confirm that they wish to live in this way. When a critical mass of these individuals is reached, the vast majority will then transform to live in higher consciousness.

Future Earth: As disclosed earlier in this Part IV, Earth was originally created as the "Jewel of the Universe." It remained in the gaseous state of a Christed 12th Dimension planet for several billion years. During this time, beings from around this universe visited this beautiful planet to experience what it offered and to take that experience back to their home planets as an example.

After the Great Cataclysm, the Fall of Consciousness, Earth was restarted with the goal of resurrecting it to once again be that wonderful planet of long ago. The humans of Earth were chosen as the mechanism by which this will take place. Nonphysicals have seen the reality of a resurrected Earth. This, they have assured us, will happen.

What lies between here and that distant goal of a 12th Dimension planet is a chasm defined by how quickly humanity will choose to raise its consciousness, thereby raising the consciousness of the planet.

At this moment we have a planet in dense physical form. We have a human population that is operating at a mixture of 3rd, 4th and 5th Dimensions, with the majority in various levels of 4th Dimension. The next step is to watch the result of the infusion of Christ Consciousness and how it will get a significant portion of humanity to function at the 5th Dimension.

As I have stated before, extrapolating new ways or new technologies arising from the conventional paradigm will not achieve this goal. Extraterrestrials are not coming to rescue humanity. We will continue to get assistance from non-humans, but it is clearly up to us to move the process forward. I know it will be much easier after the infusion of Christ Consciousness.

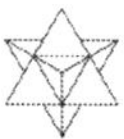

Envision future Earth as a 5th Dimension, semi-physical Earth with semi-physical human beings living on it. The human body has been changed to hold the energy of 5th Dimension, as has the planet. There are no remnants of 3rd Dimension.

There is no solid ground upon which to walk, no solid structures, and no assaults to the planet. Human beings no longer live with fear, violence, judgment, and the polarity associated with the 3rd Dimension. There are no governments, no money and no automobiles.

Manifesting whatever they desire fulfills the needs of individual human beings. Unconditional Love is the basis for everyday living. Each human is in perfect Unity with every other human, as well as every aspect of the planet. There is peace, harmony and fulfillment among all. Earth is once again a Christed planet, bathed in the uplifting energy of Christ Consciousness.

Visitors from all planets of the universe will come to Earth to see what has been accomplished, to see the success of Earth humans. Once again Earth will emit the beautiful light of higher consciousness and shine like a star with that energy.

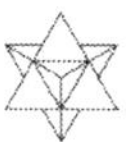

Influence: *You can influence others by walking away from the 3rd Dimension: anger, judgment, separation, less than, and domination. You can influence others by raising your energy, and by embracing who you really are. You can influence others by knowing the Cosmic*

Paradigm in all of its vastness and beauty. You can influence others by broadcasting your energy as you go about your daily life. This is much more than meditating, and then returning to your conventional life. What I am proposing is living every hour of every day, as who you really are, a higher consciousness person.

All this is easy, once you determine that you wish to be on this path. It is private. You do not need to stand on the street corner, write books, or make speeches. Yes, you can influence many by being who you really are, a Divine individual expression and a collective expression, who manifests Christ Consciousness.

I am learning to live in the 5th Dimension. Occasionally, I slip back into 4th Dimension, when I get irritated, fearful of what comes next, or worry about something. I know when this happens and I set out to center myself once again in unconditional Love and perfect Unity.

Where we are: I used to see that the ascension of humanity to the 5th Dimension would take some time, maybe fifty or a hundred years. It could happen sooner, but I was not counting on that. Then came the incredible collective of Christ Consciousness that I referenced before, and their proposed infusion of Christ Energy into every human. I am now seeing that the ascension of humanity can happen more quickly.

For me, it is enough to know that I am making a difference in the most important event in the history of humanity, an event that will be known throughout the universe.

Now that you have read this book, I hope that you will join me and push toward making Earth a 12th Dimension Christed planet of Light, Love and Unity. We may not be in these bodies for the final act, but we surely will know when the inevitable occurs. And who knows, we may decide to come back for a visit, or to stay for a while in a new lifetime.

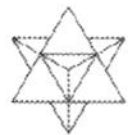

The following message, that I transcribed, speaks for itself:

Good Morning, Mark.

We come to you this day as ultraterrestrials who are present in Andromeda. We are a collective and do not manifest an individual presence. You may address us as Andromedan Ultraterrestrials.

Good morning to you, Andromedan Ultraterrestrials.

For sake of clarification, those who are aboard Athabantian are individual manifestations of various collectives present in the Galaxy of Andromeda. The collectives there are of various designs and levels of experience and consciousness. Those who are aboard Athabantian have manifested an individuality, so that they might communicate with you. You have found it convenient to address them as individuals, even though they are expressing individuality only for the purpose of communicating with you. All aboard Athabantian function as a collective. They manifest individuality only when desired.

Thank you, that is most helpful.

Now we wish to convey to you the following message. Your soul individuated itself for your life on Earth. We encouraged you to do this. You carry with you the imprint of many lifetimes in Andromeda. This imprint makes it possible for us to communicate this day. Moreover, you are now functioning, as an anchor for Andromedan energy on planet Earth. This is a most valuable linkage for us to focus our energies.

The ascension of Earth to a 12th Dimension Christed planet of Light is assured. However, it will require many years, possibly hundreds of years. First, there is the step of raising all to the 5th Dimension. We foresee that event. We foresee the final return of Earth to 12th Dimension. We do not see when, because for us time does not exist.

Our energies are very powerful. Since the resurrection of Earth, we have depended on those in star systems in your galaxy to transmute our energies to a lower frequency so that they might be usable by those of you on the planet. The step of creating Athabantian and populating it with a collective from Andromeda was a major step for increasing the Light available to your planet.

The individual beings who you call Justine, Moraine, Bren-Ton, Adrial, and Caltous are of your creation, are due to your need to believe you are receiving messages from an individual like yourself.

Each of them has told you that they were part of a collective, but with your former lower state of consciousness, you assumed that they were like you, and you gave them human-like characteristics and names. They did not manifest as individuals, you saw them as individuals because that is what was familiar to you. We are telling you this because, as Earth ascends, those who remain on the planet will become enclosed first into collectives and then into Unity. They will no longer function as individuals, as you know individuals to be. This is a far step beyond what is in your immediate future.

In your immediate future is a body accommodating higher and higher consciousness. Your physical body has already been modified to hold the consciousness that you now have. This process will continue. And as that process continues, your imprinted soul will become more and more comfortable with your body. Then you will speak out as to who you really are.

At the same time, you will find that you long to become part of a collective such as you have already experienced in the 7th Dimension.

In that higher vibration you felt loved, relaxed and integrated with all. This is the feeling you long to return to. This feeling of great peace is where those aboard Athabantian reside. This feeling of complete Unity and Love is where we, who are of the ultraterrestrial realm, exist. But there is much more to who we are and how we exist that I cannot give you words to describe.

Now go with me. Sink into that loving space. Let it envelope you. Feel the warmth and softness ....

This is your journey. This is the place we wish you to convey to others, to assist them in knowing the goal for which they came to this lifetime.

We are totally committed to the resurrection of Earth, for every moment it remains in the lower consciousness, our galaxy is impacted. Earth is but a small planet, Andromeda is a very large galaxy. However, just as a small wound to your body impacts your whole body, so does the low frequency of Earth impact all of the Milky Way Galaxy, and in turn the Andromeda Galaxy.

We applaud you, Mark, for the difficult journey you have undertaken in your dedication to the transformation of Earth. We will continue to support you energetically.

I see that you have a question about 15th Dimension. Let me say that it is neither a place nor a time, it simply is. In a human body you cannot fully comprehend it. Know that it is like a gaseous state but one with form. Those who are a part of it reside as collective energy only.

For clarification, not all in Andromeda are Ultraterrestrials. There are many levels of consciousness from 15th Dimension and above. We Ultraterrestrials, who are attached to Andromeda, exist at the highest level of Christ Consciousness, in perfect Unity with

Source. All of Andromeda is with Christ Consciousness, as well as the energy of the Holy Spirit.

We see what you have presented in this book to be generally in agreement with what we know to be true given the limits of language. We thank you for your efforts.

We see your ability to hold our energy is fading. Our blessings, Mark, you are beloved to we Ultraterrestrials of Andromeda.

Thank you. My blessings to all.

I recommend the following for additional ways to further your path to higher consciousness:

http://www.cosmicparadigm.com/
https://www.wisdomcourses.net/
https://joanandjohnwalker.com/
http://www.masteringalchemy.com/
http://www.truedivinenature.com/
http://www.starchildglobal.com/
http://www.matthewbooks.com/matthews-messages/
https://www.paths2empowerment.com/steve-barbara-rother/
http://tomkenyon.com/hathors-archives

ACKNOWLEDGMENTS

I would like to acknowledge those individuals, human and non-human, who have made a lasting impact on who I am today. They took a shy boy and matured him into a man, husband, father, writer, teacher, channel and wayshower. That I am a happy man is largely due to their positive influences.

I offer many thanks to my wife Heidi, who has been my companion, lover and constant support during the years of my maturation.

The following have been, and in many cases continue to be, my mentors and teachers. They appear in chronological order: Earl "Kim" Kimmel, Gerry Kimmel, Elmer Drake, Bee J. Drake, Jerry Heibel, Merle Ackerman, Jack Savidge, John Boyle, Tom McGeary, Chet Winter, Paul Haber, Dr. Steven Greer, Justine, Moraine, Adrial, Jim Self, Joan Walker, John Walker, Yeshua, and Archangel Michael. My gratitude to each of them for they have greatly helped me along my journey.

There have been a number of other people who have come into my life. These have provided significant challenges from which I have learned much. My thanks to each of them.

I wish to thank those who have helped with the preparation of this book. I have had support and editing critique from several special friends, both human and non-physical. I honor the fine work that Annie Miller has done in converting my manuscript into the book you have before you, plus the design of its cover.

It has been my great privilege to work on this book in conjunction with many non-humans. I am most grateful for their support, their insights, and their words as we joined together to create the finished product.

Mark Kimmel

Mark has spoken at international forums, been a guest on radio and television shows, and has conducted workshops based on his unique insights into the transformation of Earth and his interactions with the non-physical. Mark's earlier books, *Trillion, Decimal, One, Birthing A New Civilization, Transformation, Transformation, Chrysalis* and *ICEBREAKERS,* contain messages from non-human sources such as extraterrestrials, celestials, and Archangels. His new book, *Cosmic Paradigm,* contains his many experiences with non-physical beings and channelings with them.

By focusing on both extraterrestrials and Archangels in his writing and speaking, Mark weaves a credible picture of the larger reality while presenting an uplifting vision for the future of humanity and of our planet. Mark avoids the sensational and fear-riddled perspectives that plague many who deal with the ET phenomena, and the secrecy and misinformation surrounding it. He presents his contacts with Archangels and other nonphysicals without a religious orientation.

Mark's passion for writing and teaching about ETs and non-physicals is far different than his earlier career as a successful businessman, where he worked for major corporations and founded and ran three of the most respected Colorado venture capital funds. He retired from business in 1996 to pursue his quest into the larger aspects of our existence. Mark has been listed in *Who's Who* since 1985. He has degrees in engineering, marketing, finance, psychology, and divinity.

Mark is married with two grown sons and five grandchildren. He spends his days writing and speaking about this, the pivotal juncture in human history, and how each person has the power to impact all on this planet by living at higher consciousness. He is the founder of the Cosmic Paradigm Network, an international group dedicated to manifesting Earth's transformation.

CONTACT for Mark Kimmel

Email: CP@zqyx.org

Web Site: http://www.cosmicparadigm.com/

Made in the USA
San Bernardino, CA
25 April 2018